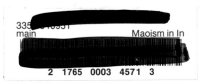

P9-DKD-413

MAOISM IN INDIA

MAOISM
in
INDIA

MOHAN RAM

BARNES & NOBLE, Inc.

NEW YORK

PUBLISHERS & BOOKSELLERS SINCE 1873

First Published in the United States, 1971
by Barnes & Noble, Inc.

ISBN 389   04198   x

335.4340951
R 165m
1971

PRINTED IN THE UNITED STATES OF AMERICA

PREFACE

THERE ARE several nuances to the fragmented Indian Maoist movement. In the absence of any term that describes them adequately, Indian Maoists have come to be called "Naxalites" after the 1967 peasant uprising in Naxalbari, a 270-square mile enclave in West Bengal. But Naxalbari is neither the beginning nor the end of Indian Maoism and Maoist armed struggle in India. The terms "Naxalite" and "Naxalism" is now debased political coinage, used indiscriminately by the detractors and opponents of Maoism.

Indian Maoism predates the final victory of the Chinese Revolution in 1949. In its first appearance, it was a short-lived phenomenon of the late 1940s and was suppressed by international intervention. After nearly two decades, it has returned in a changed context.

The last three years have witnessed the extensive growth of the Maoist movement in India, despite the set-backs and the fragmentation it has suffered. To a whole generation of idealist youth, the Maoist movement represents the quest for something meaningful and relevant, outside the parliamentary system whose legitimacy is becoming increasingly doubtful.

This study is a follow-up on my earlier book, *Indian Communism—Split Within a Split*,* which had attempted an analysis of the Indian communist developments culminating in the return of Maoism to India. The response was overwhelming though the book itself was imperfect and inadequate in many respects. The need for a comprehensive study of the Indian Maoist movement remained. Here is a little attempt to meet it.

India has a central place in the Maoist strategy of people's war commended to the Third World. The Indian commu-

* Vikas Publications, Delhi, 1969.

nist movement has been the battleground of the Sino-Soviet
ideological dispute on issues like peaceful transition to
socialism and the concept of national democracy which are
patently Soviet innovations, considered revisionist by the
Chinese leadership.

This book tries to place India in the Maoist strategy and
trace the evolution of the Chinese line for India leading to
the call for a Maoist revolution in mid-1967, as part of the
general strategy of people's war for the Third World. Naxalbari provided the occasion for vigorous reassertion of the
Maoist model.

But the present phase of the Maoist movement had a
faltering start, with a Maoist party formed from above without regard to the problem of evolving a tactical line. The
Communist Party of India (Marxist-Leninist), formed in
1969, began without either a programme or a constitution
and has been groping for a tactical line. The Communist
Party of China has recognized this as India's only legitimate
communist party but significantly has neither denounced
nor recognized the other Maoist formations in the country.

The Chinese leadership has to contend with two shades
of Maoism in India, represented by the divergent tactical
lines of CPI(M) and the Andhra Pradesh Revolutionary
Communist Committee. The tactical line blessed by the
Chinese leadership has lapsed into group terrorism with no
relation to any mass movement because the line is based on
a patently non-Maoist philosophy of armed struggle, rejecting both mass participation and the role of mass organizations. No wonder the CPI(M-L)'s leadership of the
Srikakulam movement in Andhra Pradesh (which predates
Naxalbari by almost a decade) has resulted in its virtual
liquidation.

The alternative focus is provided by the Andhra Maoists
who have the benefit of the lessons of Telengana peasant
struggle of 1946-51. The tactical line worked by the Andhra

Maoists appears to be a creative application of Maoism to India while the CPI(M-L) has been very mechanical in its approach to the problems of "people's war."

The book attempts an examination of all these issues and assesses the potential of a Maoist revolution in India.

The author has no pretension to scholarship and no claims to authority. At best, the book has a story to tell by a journalist who has reported it as it developed.

The author's debt in this effort is to many. But most of is to the friendly staff of the School of International Studies library where much of the research was done, to several friends who helped with advice and rare material but would not like to be identified, and, of course. to Mr. S. Swaminathan who had to grapple with a near-impossible manuscript.

MOHAN RAM

CONTENTS

CHAPTER ONE

INDIA IN MAOIST STRATEGY

THE COMMUNIST PARTY of China's call in June-July 1967 for armed revolutions in India, Burma, and Indonesia marked a new stage in the Sino-Soviet ideological struggle. It was a collision of two different attitudes to the role of national liberation movement when the Vietnam war had become the focal point of all the contradictions of the epoch. To the Communist Party of the Soviet Union, the contradiction between the socialist camp and imperialism was almost the only global contradiction while the Communist Party of China identified the one between the oppressed nations and imperialism as the foremost. By transferring the struggle against imperialism to the Third World, the Chinese were trying to challenge anew, on a higher plane, the Soviet ideological positions on peaceful coexistence, peaceful competition, and peaceful transition, and rejecting the suggestion for "unity in action" in Vietnam. Three countries where the Soviet Union saw the most chance of peaceful transition to socialism and whose regimes the Soviet Union and the United States were underwriting with economic aid and diplomatic support were chosen by the CPC for implementation of its new strategy for the Third World.

The strategy of people's war based on guerilla tactics proposed by Lin Piao on 2 September 1965 in his famous article

"Long Live the Victory of People's War" was a vigorous reassertion of the Maoist model of revolution for the Third World. Along with this article, to mark the twentieth anniversary of China's war against Japan, two other articles on the same day, one by Lo Jui-ching (in *People's Daily*) and the other, a *People's Daily* editorial, stressed the importance of people's war. The three articles were part of the foreign policy debate that had begun early in 1965 in the Communist Party of China. It was not until after Mao Tse-tung had supported Lin Piao's thesis that it could win decisively at the Eleventh Plenary Session of the Central Committee[1] in August 1966.

Lin's strategy commended Mao's theory of people's war as the "common asset of the revolutionary people of the whole world" because it had "characteristics of our epoch." Whether one wanted a tit-for-tat struggle against imperialist armed aggression or suppression or a fight against it was tantamount to whether one dared embark on a revolution. This was the best touchstone to tell the genuine revolutionaries from the fake ones. Mao's theory of people's war solved not only the problems of people's war but also those of waging it. His theory of rural revolutionary bases was "outstanding and universal and of practical importance" to Asia, Africa, and Latin America which constituted the rural areas of the world while the North American and West European capitalist countries constituted the cities. The Chinese revolution had solved the problem of linking up the national democratic with socialist revolution in the colonial and semi-colonial countries. Mao's was a "complete

---

[1] For a detailed account of the internal conflict on global policy in the Communist Party of China which culminated in the victory for the Mao Tse-tung-Lin Piao line, see Uri Ra'anan, "Peking's Foreign Policy Debate," in Tang Tsou (Ed.), *China in Crisis*, Volume II, University of Chicago, 1968.

theory of new democratic revolution" against imperialism, feudalism, and bureaucratic capitalism waged "by the broad masses of people under the leadership of the proletariat." Lin's strategy aimed at linking all the people's wars in the Third World into a global front against United States, reinforcing each other and merging into a "torrential worldwide tide."[2]

Besides, United States imperialism itself was divisible and could be destroyed bit by bit through people's wars in the Third World. When United States imperialism was dreading people's war most, the "Khrushchev revisionists" came to its rescue by debunking it and "scheming to undermine" it, Lin said. The revisionists had no faith in the masses, had succumbed to the United States nuclear blackmail, and were afraid that people's war for the fight of the socialist countries against U.S. agression would involve them in a conflict that would smash the dreams of the Soviet-United States cooperation to dominate the world. Lin challenged the Soviet theory that a nation without nuclear weapons cannot defeat an enemy with nuclear weapons and ridiculed the belief that a single spark anywhere would touch off a world nuclear confrontation. People's war was the answer to all the issues in the changed strategic environment.

Lin's thesis was thus also a frontal attack on the Soviet ideological positions and the general line of the "three peacefuls"[3]—peaceful coexistence, peaceful competition, and peaceful transition. The strategy aimed at a combined onslaught on U.S. imperialism and Soviet revisionism in the Third World through an escalation of the national liberation movement.

[2] Lin Piao, "Long Live The Victory of People's War," People's Daily, 2 September 1965; Peking Review, 3 September 1965.
[3] Ibid.

Though the people's war strategy for the Third World had won acceptance at the Central Committee plenum in August 1966 (that is, two months before the Cultural Revolution reached its climax), it took the CPC another year to call for its implementation, almost simultaneously, in India, Burma, and Indonesia, in that order. Preoccupation with the Cultural Revolution might not have been the sole reason for the significant lag of about a year.

By mid-1967, India had gone through its fourth general elections and new governments had taken office at the federal level and in the States. The Communist Party of India (Marxist), formed in 1964 following the split in the pro-Moscow Communist Party of India, persisted in its equivocation on peaceful transition and the parliamentary path. When the CPI(M) found itself participating in non-ideological coalition ministries in Kerala and West Bengal, the CPC was far from pleased with the behaviour of the only communist party it recognized in India. China's state-level relations with Burma had deteriorated to a new low by mid-1967 and the Ne Win government had moved closer to the Soviet Union. In Indonesia, Suharto had come to stay. The coup in October 1965 had underlined the failure of the Indonesian Communist Party's line of reliance on peaceful transition and on Sukarno. Though the party, decimated as a result of the post-coup massacre, had analyzed its mistakes as early as August 1966, the CPC published it only in July 1967 to synchronize with its call for armed revolution in Indonesia. It is possible that the CPC had hoped that Sukarno could still pull it off but when he was formally deposed in May 1967, a new strategy was called for. This might be the reason for the delayed publication of the Indonesian party documents. Publication of these documents in Peking meant the CPC's approval of them.

The developments in India, Burma, and Indonesia in the aggregate warranted, in the CPC's view, a new, coordinated strategy to secure the defeat of the peaceful transition line and to shift the struggle against the United States and the ideological struggle against Soviet Union to the Third World.

New Strategic Environment

Before it went about implementing the new Third World strategy by calling for Maoist revolutions in India, Burma, and Indonesia in June-July 1967, the Chinese leadership appeared to have made a fresh assessment of the world revolutionary potential. As late as July 1966, the emphasis was on the Third World support to the Vietnamese struggle for defeating U.S. imperialism. The Afro-Asian Writers' Emergency Meeting in Peking on 9 July 1966 reflected the Chinese thinking adequately. It adopted 37 resolutions supporting armed struggles in Asia and Africa. The principal task of the Afro-Asian peoples was identified as the elimination of all forces and influences of imperialism and colonialism in the political, economic, and cultural domains and the carrying through to the end of the national liberation struggle. U.S. imperialism was described as the most ferocious enemy of the people of the Third World, and of the world as a whole,[4] and the Soviet Union its accomplice because it was striving to "undermine the solidarity and the revolutionary cause of the Afro-Asian people" and had "placed itself in antagonism with the Afro-Asian people and

---

[4] Communique of the Afro-Asian Writers' Emergency Meeting, Peking, 9 July; *Peking Review*, 15 July 1966.

the people of the world."[5]

Early in 1967, the CPC saw a qualitative change in the world revolutionary situation alongside an attempt by the United States, with Soviet help, for an anti-China *cordon sanitaire*. A review of 1966 began with a Mao thought: "We are now in a great new era of world revolution. The revolutionary upheaval in Asia, Africa, and Latin America is sure to deal the whole of the old world a decisive and crushing blow."

The review said that U.S. imperialism helped by Soviet revisionists had increasingly shifted the emphasis of its counter-revolutionary global strategy from Europe to Asia and was attempting to stamp out the flames of Asian peoples' struggle, particularly in Vietnam. Alongside, the peoples of Asia, "influenced and inspired by Mao Tse-tung's Thought" were waging a united struggle. Besides the armed struggle in Vietnam, Laos, and Thailand, "the people have carried on mass political struggle, including armed struggle against U.S. imperialism and its lackeys" in a number of countries. Armed struggle was "unabated" in Philippines. In India, "the mass movement against the reactionary Congress Government swept the entire country....This movement has broken out of the bonds of economic struggle and once dominant doctrine of 'non-violence' is becoming increasingly discredited." In Indonesia, it was a "sustained struggle" against the rightist military regime despite the 1965 bloodbath. In Japan, it was "tit-for-tat struggle" against the followers of Soviet revisionists.[6]

It was, on the whole, a "gloomy new year" for imperialism because the "revolutionary storm of the world's people" was

[5] "The Militant Banner of Afro-Asian Solidarity is Flying High," Editorial, *People's Daily*, 10 July; *Peking Review*, 15 July 1966.
[6] "Great New Era of World Revolution," *Peking Review*, 13 January 1967.

sweeping forward quickening the disintegration of the imperialist camp headed by the United States. "The day of their burial is not far off."[7] But the United States-Soviet collusion against China was broadening.[8]

By mid-1967, the revolutionary situation had turned "excellent" amidst sharper international class struggle, with more revolutionary wars and counter-revolutionary wars than eight years ago. "The world is full of the smell of gunpowder," wrote the *People's Daily* and the commentary, "To Hell with the Theory of 'Dying out' of Wars!" reflected Chinese optimism and confidence. Alexei Kosygin's call for "an end to the war" at that juncture, the commentary said, was aimed at greater United States-Soviet collusion against people's revolutionary struggle.[9]

India, Burma, and Indonesia

This was the new strategic environment in which the CPC called for armed revolutions in India, Burma and Indonesia, and it was the new strategy in action. A peasant revolt led by the extremists of the Communist Party of India (Marxist) in Naxalbari, in Darjeeling district of West Bengal, where the party shared power at the State level, provided the occasion for spelling out the Maoist strategy for India. A *People's Daily* article credited to a "Red Guard," broadcast by Radio Peking on 10 June, called for "relentless armed struggle" to overthrow the Indian government and "forcibly seize power."

The Chinese saw in the Naxalbari revolt the first spark of

[7] "Imperialist Camp Enters Gloomy New Year," *Peking Review*, 20 January 1967.

[8] *Peking Review*, 10 February 1967.

[9] *Radio Peking*, 1 July 1967.

revolutionary armed struggle that could start a prairie fire in India. Naxalbari represented "the general orientation of the Indian revolution at the present time. The people of India, China, and the rest of the world hail the emergence of this revolutionary armed struggle."[10]

In Burma, open support to armed struggle and a call to overthrow the Ne Win Government followed deterioration in the state-level relations. The shift came on 30 June 1967, after China, following anti-Chinese riots, had decided that its ambassador would not return to Rangoon. *People's Daily* denounced the Ne Win regime which it said had seized power through a military coup and had discarded "the fig leaf of bourgeois democracy" and "clamped down a military fascist rule." Revolutionary armed struggle led by the Communist Party of Burma was developing successfully and in the past year in particular, it had grown much stronger taking the national democratic revolution an important step further.[11] Significantly, no reference had been made to armed struggle in Burma in the review of the revolutionary situation in 1966,[12] but *People's Daily* was now referring to the growth of the armed struggle during the past year in particular.

From now on, attacks on the Burmese regime from Peking were more frequent. On 5 July, Thakin Ba Thein Tin, First Vice-chairman of the Communist Party of Burma, told a memorial rally in Peking for the Chinese technical expert Liu Yi killed in Rangoon, that this incident was part of the anti-China drive in Indonesia, India, Hong Kong, and in other countries and was carried out in collusion with

[10] NCNA, Peking, 27 June 1967.
[11] "The Burmese Government Must Stop All anti-Chinese Atrocities," *People's Daily*, 30 June 1967, NCNA translation.
[12] See fn. 7 supra.

United States imperialism, Soviet revisionism, world reaction, and Kuomintang bandit gangs.[13]

This was followed by a commentary which explained the Ne Win regime's anti-China stance as the invitable result of class struggle and the growing strength of the revolutionary armed forces. The path of Burma's revolution was no longer in doubt:

> The armed struggle led by the Communist Party of Burma...represents the direction of the historical development of Burma. The people of all nationalities throughout Burma...are now, under the leadership of the Communist Party of Burma, closing their ranks more tightly in rebellion against the Ne Win Government and this is taking the form of a revolutionary people's war.[14]

About the same time, the CPC called for the overthrow of the regime in Indonesia. Radio Peking devoted its bulletins on 2 and 8 July to an analysis or the Communist Party of Indonesia's mistakes since 1945, its Politbureau's statement of 17 August 1966 and the Politbureau's self-criticism of September 1966. The statement had said that the party's task was to build itself as a Marxist-Leninist party opposed to modern revisionism to be able to lead a protracted armed struggle integrated with agrarian revolution, and to form a united front of all forces opposed to the military regime. The self-criticism said that during the last 15 years, the party had got bogged down in parliamentary and other forms of legal struggle. In sum, it lost its independence in the united front with the national bourgeoisie.

[13] NCNA, Peking, 5 July 1967.
[14] "By Frenziedly Opposing China, the Ne Win Reactionary Government is Inviting its Own Doom," *People's Daily* editorial, 10 July 1967.

The authoritative *Red Flag* said that the Indonesian party
faced a difficult task because it had to switch from cities to
the countryside, from peaceful struggle to armed struggle and
from legal to illegal and from open to secret activity. But
the objective realities of the revolutionary struggle would
compel people to make the change, compel them to master
armed struggle because there was no alternative to it. The
CPC pledged support to the Indonesian revolution in unmistakable terms:

> We stand unflinchingly on the side of the PKI, on the
> side of the Indonesian revolutionary people, and firmly
> support the struggle waged by the PKI in leading the
> Indonesian people to overthrow the Suharto-Nasutian
> fascist regime.... [15]

Thus in June-July 1967, the CPC had prescribed people's
war as the answer to the problems of national democratic
revolution in India, Burma, and Indonesia. The order in
which these countries received the CPC's attention was
significant. In India it synchronized with Naxalbari uprising. In Burma, it coincided with China's belligerence
abroad leading to strained relations even with friendly countries like Nepal and Ceylon and the Vijay-Raghunath incident in Peking with India. The strain in relations with
Burma and Indonesia was over the people of Chinese origin.

Peaceful Transition, the Issue

This was roughly the time when the Cultural Revolution
extended to foreign relations. To what extent the change

15 NCNA, 8 July 1967.

in attitude to the Indian, Burmese, and Indonesian regimes was a function of the struggle against Liu Shao-chi is hard to tell. But there are several references to "China's Khrushchev" in the attacks on the peaceful transition line.

There was also an attempt to fix the responsibility on Liu Shao-chi for China's mistaken prettification of the Ne Win regime. An authoritative article said in the past, thanks to the "assiduous glorification" of the regime by the Soviet revisionists and China's Khrushchev, "not a few people had an impression that this regime was somehow 'progressive'."[16]

The CPC's effort in India was directed at securing a shift in the tactical line of the Communist Party of India (Marxist), which had equivocated on armed struggle, like the Moscow-backed Communist Party of India, taken the parliamentary path.

The CPC approvingly published an article by a Burmese communist leader to mark the 28th anniversary of his party. It sought to snipe at Liu Shao-chi and to debunk what it called the Indian road to revolution.

The Soviet Khrushchevian revisionists and China's Khrushchev and his gang have time and again tried to make us abandon China's road and take India's road. They said Burma was not like old China. In Burma, there was more bourgeois democracy than in old China ruled by the Chiang Kai-shek regime and it was possible to make use of bourgeois democracy in waging struggle. Their aim was to make us abandon armed struggle, enter into the legal orbit and engage in long-term legal struggle.[17]

[16] "Be Armed With Mao Tse-tung's Thought to Strike Down Our Common Enemy," *People's Daily*, 10 July 1967.

[17] Thakin Ba Thien Tin, "Burmese People's Revolutionary Armed Struggle is Bound to Triumph," *Peking Review*, 1 September 1967.

India, and more especially the form of its transition to socialism, has been crucial to the CPC's alternative general line for the international communist movement. Peaceful transition through the parliamentary process was a Khrushchevian innovation at the 20th Congress of the Communist Party of Soviet Union in 1956. Khrushchev's concept of peaceful transition, repeated by Anastas Mikoyan and Mikhail Suslov, was in fact a corollary to his declaration that peaceful coexistence was the "general line of the Soviet policy."

The peaceful transition thesis was based on an integrated strategy. In the changed international environment, the powerful socialist bloc could provide the supporting base of world revolution and by interacting with the local progressive forces outside, bring about a new correlation of forces to make peaceful transition possible. Two features of the new environment—the emergence of a vast Peace Zone in Asia and the degree of economic and diplomatic support the socialist camp can give to prevent its rapprochment with the West were central to the strategy. The transition, as visualized by the Soviet leadership, involved three stages. This was how Khrushchev outlined it. The working class, by rallying itself and other forces was in a position to defeat the forces opposed to the popular interest, to capture majority in parliament and transform it into a genuine instrument of the people's will.

The winning of a stable parliamentary majority backed by a mass revolutionary movement of the proletariat and of all the working people could create for the working class of a number of capitalist and former colonial countries the conditions needed to secure fundamental social change.

In countries where capitalism is still strong and has a huge military and police apparatus at its disposal, the reactionary forces will of course inevitably offer serious resistance. There the transition to socialism will be attended by sharp, revolutionary struggle.[18]

Parliamentarism was the basis of the thesis stated by the Soviet leadership in the broadest of terms. The countries which could strive for peaceful transition were not specified. Peaceful transition was assumed to be the rule while non-peaceful transition ("sharp class, revolutionary struggle") was viewed as an exception.

To the Chinese, the thesis amounted to a "clear revision of the Marxist-Leninist teachings on the state and revolution and a clear denial of the universal significance of the road of the October Revolution." Peaceful coexistence as advocated by Khrushchev amounted, according to the CPC, to "excluding from the general line of the foreign policy of the socialist countries their mutual assistance and cooperation as well as assistance by them to the revolutionary struggles of the oppressed peoples and nations, or to subordinating all this to the policy of so-called 'peaceful coexistence'."[19]

Forms of transition to socialism and attitude to revolutionary struggles of the Third World have been among the issues of the Sino-Soviet ideological dispute, one phase of which culminated in the alternative Chinese general line of

[18] N. S. Khrushchev, *Report of the Central Committee of the Communist Party of Soviet Union to the XX Party Congress, February 14, 1956*, Moscow, 1956, pp. 42-6.

[19] Editorial Departments of *People's Daily* and *Red Flag*, "The Origin and Development of Differences Between the Leadership of the CPSU and Ourselves: Comment on the Open Letter of the Central Committee of the CPSU — 1," *Peking Review*, 13 September 1963.

the international communist movement.[20] The Sino-Soviet
ideological dispute can be said to have had its origins in
the Soviet formulations at the 20th Congress of the CPSU.
In fact, one of the minor issues related to the Congress itself.

While the CPSU claims that the CPC had accepted the
thesis but had made a "180-degree turn" in its evaluation of
the 20th CPSU Congress,[21] the CPC maintains that it had
always differed "in its view of the 20th Congress" and "the
leading comrades of the CPSU are aware of it."[22] It is on
record that the Chinese raised this issue once again with
the CPSU at the 1957 meeting of the representatives of the
Communist and Workers Parties in Moscow. Peaceful
transition was the main issue between the two parties and
the original draft declaration proposed by the CPSU was
modified on the Chinese insistence. The draft was silent
on non-peaceful transition and had mentioned only peaceful
transition. Besides it had described peaceful transition as
"securing a majority in parliament" and transforming it
"from an instrument of the bourgeois dictatorship into an
instrument of genuine people's state power." The CPC
opposed this and expressed its reservations on two successive drafts of the CPSU. A revised draft put forward by the
CPC provided the basis of discussions between the two
delegations before the "Joint Draft Declaration by the
CPSU and the CPC" was circulated among other delegations. The declaration in its final form (on 16 November

[20] "A Proposal Concerning the General Line of the International
Communist Movement," CC, CPC, 14 June 1963.

[21] CPSU Central Committee, "Open Letter to its Party Organizations at all Levels and to All its Party Members," Soviet News, 16
July 1963.

[22] Editorial Departments of People's Daily and Red Flag, "The
Origin and Development...," loc. cit.

1957) made two major changes on the question of transition from capitalism to socialism compared with the first draft proposed by CPSU. One, the declaration besides indicating the possibility of peaceful transition, referred to non-peaceful transition and asserted that "Leninism teaches, and experience confirms, that the ruling classes never relinquish power voluntarily." Secondly, in connection with securing "a firm majority in parliament," the declaration emphasized the need to wage "extra-parliamentary mass struggle, smash the resistance of the reactionary forces and create the necessary conditions for peaceful realisation of the socialist revolution."

Though the CPC was not satisfied with these changes it "conceded the point" because the leaders of the CPSU had pleaded that the formulation should have some connection with that of the 20th Congress.[23] The CPC's own views on the question were stated in the note "Outline of Views on the Question of Peaceful Transition."[24] Briefly the CPC's position was: It would be more flexible to refer to both peaceful and non-peaceful because that would leave the political initiative with the communists but referring only to peaceful transition would tie their hands; it might be tactically advantageous to refer to peaceful transition but it would be inappropriate to overemphasize its possibility; to the best of their knowledge there was still "not a country where this possibility is of any practical significance"; should such possibility arise the Communists could always take advantage of it; to obtain majority in parliament was not the same as smashing the old state machinery and establishing the new state machinery; peaceful transition to socialism

[23] *Ibid.*
[24] Appendix to *ibid.*

should not be interpreted in such a way that it solely means transition through parliamentary majority.[25]

India, the Testing Ground

Though neither the 20th CPSU Congress nor the Moscow declaration had specified the countries that held out possibilities of peaceful transition, there was little doubt that the Soviet leadership saw greatest chances of such transition in India. One of the main postulates of the Soviet strategy (economic and diplomatic support to the countries of the Peace Zone in Asia to prevent their alignment with the West) had been tried with measurable success in India and was already part of Soviet experience. The CPI had already been persuaded to accept the strategy.

In the wake of the disastrous 1948 Zhdanov line of insurrections in South-East Asia and amidst the changed needs of a cold war situation, the Soviet leadership decided in 1951 to replace class struggle by cold war. The Communist Party of India (CPI) swung from right reformism, most pronounced at the time of Independence (August 1947) to left sectarianism early in 1948 (Calcutta congress) and believed in the Titoite theory of intertwining of the two stages of revolution, assuming that India was already a capitalist country. In 1950, on international intervention, it abandoned the Calcutta line and switched to the Maoist strategy of a four-class alliance for a two-stage revolution. Soviet intervention in 1951 forced the party to shelve, if not abandon, armed struggle as a tactic and settle for peaceful constitutionalism beginning with participation in the country's first general elections in 1952. In 1953, the main controversy

[25] *Ibid.*

in the party related to the identification of the main enemy—
British imperialism, which still dominated the Indian economy or American imperialism, which was the enemy of the
communist parties the world over. Soviet intervention
through the British communists achieved the desired shift
and the fight against British imperialism was compromised
to suit to Soviet cold war requirements. The CPI equivocated, calling for simultaneous struggles against both the im-
perialisms and in practice lined up behind the government
of Jawaharlal Nehru. The Soviet leadership was placating
him to stablize his "nonalignment" and prevent its lapse
into alignment with the Western camp.[26] Soviet Union
wanted a worldwide peace front and the CPI was to exert
pressure on Nehru to bring him into the front. The Soviet
leadership no longer regarded nonalignment a dirty word
because Nehru had shown signs of independence of the
Western camp.

The CPI, already absorbed into the Indian parliamentary
system, no wonder gave at its Third (Madurai) Congress in
1953 the central slogan of a "government of democratic
unity." Left unity was to be the precondition for democratic unity because its preoccupation was with an anti-Ame-
rican peace front designed to help Moscow. General
Secretary Ajoy Ghosh noted two conflicting trends at the
congress. One saw in the United States only a threat to
peace and not to freedom. The other saw the United
States as the only enemy to be fought for both peace and

---

[26] A detailed account of these developments can be found in
Gene D. Overstreet and Marshal Windmiller, *Communism in India*,
California University, 1959; John H. Kautsky, *Moscow and the
Communist Party of India*, Wiley and MIT, New York and Cam-
bridge, 1956; and Mohan Ram, *Indian Communism: Split Within
a Split*, Vikas, Delhi, 1969.

national liberation. But "the struggle for peace and the struggle for national liberation are not identical or coextensive,"[27] Ghosh said. All those who struggled for completion of India's freedom had to join the peace front but all those fighting for peace did not have to join the struggle for full freedom. Logically, the emphasis was to be on a broad-based peace front, the struggle for full freedom taking the back seat.

The CPI found itself supporting Nehru's foreign policy which was showing an anti-West orientation. When the United States entered an arms pact with Pakistan in February 1954, Nehru declared that "the countries of Asia and certainly India do not accept this policy and do not propose to be dominated by any country." Soviet Premier G. M. Melankov hailed "India's great contribution to the cause of peace."[28] Nehru moved closer to the socialist camp, calling for end to bomb tests, and taking initiative on the Korean problem. In June 1954, Chinese Premier Chou En-lai visited New Delhi and together with Nehru enunciated the famous Five Principles (Panchsheel) of peaceful coexistence which the Soviet leadership was to support later.

With Soviet and Chinese support to Nehru's foreign policy, a section of the CPI leadership, under the cover of fighting "imperialist machinations in Asia," tried to commit the party's support to Nehru's domestic policies and there was a retreat even from the Madurai position. International intervention to strengthen the CPI right wing's efforts came in the form of an article by the British leader R. Palme Dutt who wanted the struggle for freedom and

[27] Ajoy Ghosh, "On the Work of the Third Party Congress," New Age, 24 January 1954.
[28] The Hindu, 2 March 1954.

the struggle for peace telescoped.[29]

Dutt's veiled directive was reinforced by direct Soviet advice through the CPI General Secretary who went to Moscow for medical attention in July. He returned in December to plead for "support to the peaceful aspects of Nehru's foreign policy."[30] Nehru's domestic policies were branded reactionary nevertheless.[31]

From now on it was a fierce struggle between the right and the left groups over the attitude to the Nehru government and the ruling Congress Party, the centrists led by Ghosh holding the balance. It was a battle for a new programme and a new tactical line culminating in an open split and the formation of the Communist Party of India (Marxist), before the CPI could replace its obsolete 1951 programme. In 1964 there were two communist parties, two programmes, and two tactical lines.

Amidst the CPI controversy, Nehru launched a drive for closer relations with the socialist bloc. He visited China in November 1954 and Soviet Union in 1955. Marshal Tito of Yugoslavia visited India in January 1955. Nehru played an important role at the Bandung Afro-Asian Conference in April 1955. Soviet leaders, Khrushchev, First Secretary of the CPSU, and Marshal Bulganin, Premier, visited India late in 1955. Indo-Soviet economic cooperation had got into stride with Soviet aid for the Bhilai steel plant and the ruling Congress Party had set itself the goal of a "socialist pattern"

[29] R. Palme Dutt, "New Features in the National Liberation Struggle of Colonial and Dependent People," *For a Lasting Peace, for a People's Democracy*, 8 October 1964; *New Age*, 14 November 1954.

[30] Ajoy Ghosh, "Communists Answer Pandit Nehru," *New Age*, 5 December 1954.

[31] "Ajoy Ghosh Answers Questions on Communist Policies," *New Age*, 12 December 1954.

of society in January 1955. Moscow began seeing progressive features not only in Nehru's foreign policies but also in his domestic policies and a *Pravda* editorial on India's Republic Day, 26 January 1955, heralded a major shift in the Soviet policy towards the Nehru Government. India was to be the pivot of the new Soviet policy for Asia, particularly the countries of the Peace Zone of which India had emerged leader. *Pravda's* praise for Nehru's policies proved disastrous for the ultra-left Andhra State unit of the party which had wrested clearance from the central leadership to force mid-term elections in the State. The Andhra communists made an ambitious bid for power on the slogan of "government of democratic unity" but their sectarian tactical line led them to defeat.

The leftist veneer of the Congress Party, and more particularly the Second Five Year Plan which embodied the government's economic policies, demanded a reassessment of the situation. The result was a compromise between total opposition to the Congress and coalition with it. The June 1955 Central Committee resolution backed Nehru's foreign policies and declared qualified support to certain features of the Plan and opposed some others.[32] It could not help seeing a progressive orientation in Nehru's domestic policies. The ultimate goal of a people's democratic governments at the federal level (to make for peaceful transition to socialism) remained. But the immediate objective was government of democratic unity in the States, conditions for which were to be created through mass struggle both supporting and opposing Nehru's policies. These struggles would snowball into a nationwide movement affecting even

[32] *Communist Party in the Struggle for Peace, Democracy and National Advance*, Communist Party of India, New Delhi, 1955.

the federal government. The CPI rejected direct cooperation with the government but did not rule out united action
with the Congress Party from below.

When the Central Committee met again in September
1955, agreement on support to Nehru's foreign policy was
evident and the differences were limited to his domestic
policies. One group attributed the left orientation in the
polices to a split in the national bourgeoisie, one section
seeking collaboration with imperialism and feudalism. Nehru
Government, which sought socialist aid as a lever for more
aid from the West, was seen as the representative of the
progressive section of the big business. The government had
abandoned collaboration with imperialism and taken to
peaceful coexistence and cooperation with the socialist camp.
The drive for industrialization aimed at liquidating semi-
colonialism, leading to economic independence. Nehru
could do this only moving nearer the camp of peace and
anti-imperialism. Therefore, the need was for a united
national front as a prelude to a "government of national
unity," which meant a coalition with Congress, an emergency alliance to resist the "pro-imperialist and pro-feudal
offensive." Another group, more explicit on this point, advanced the slogan of a "national democratic government."
The third reiterated the formulations of the 1951 programme, viz. India was a semi-colonial and dependent country
under a big bourgeois-landlord government collaborating
with British imperialism.

In December 1955, General Secretary Ghosh rejected the
plan for coalition with the Congress and in February 1965
(on the eve of the 20th CPSU Congress) outlined an alternative programme of "uniting with and struggling against"
the Congress to build a national democratic front. The
Congress as a whole was not to be brought into the front

because building it involved struggle against some of its
policies. The front was to be built on the basis of struggle
for realization of anti-imperialist and democratic tasks
through united action with progressive sections of the Congress, CPI, the Praja Socialist Party, Socialist Party, and of
all democrats and patriots. The struggle would pave the
way for a formal front with a common minimum programme, ultimately leading to a stage when the "replacement of
the existing government would become an immediate possibility and a task."[33]

Thus the CPI had settled for a strategy of peaceful transition and had anticipated the "peaceful transition" thesis of
the 20th CPSU Congress. The CPSU was formalizing and
legitimizing what was already being practised under its
guidance in India. By its support to the Nehru Government, the Soviet leadership had brought the CPI round to
supporting Nehru's policies broadly and striving for a national democratic front. The Ghosh line represented a "centrist
deviation" which was to get the seal of approval at the
Fourth (Palghat) Congress in April 1956.

Ghosh, who was a fraternal delegate at the 20th CPSU
Congress, gave a detailed interpretation of the peaceful
transition thesis to his party's Fourth Congress. The objective conditions for peaceful transition had been created
thanks to the decisive shift in the world balance of forces in
favour of the socialist bloc and it was possible for the working class and its party to secure a stable parliamentary majority not only in France and England but also in Asian
countries like India and Indonesia where even the "first
stage of People's Democracy" was possible in a peaceful way.

[33] Ajoy Ghosh, "The United Front," New Age, February 1956.
1956.

Since peaceful transition was a possibility, "every communist party in every country must strive to turn the possibility into a reality." Ghosh was faithfully reflecting Soviet thinking and the Chinese had not yet raised the issue of non-peaceful transition. Outlining the CPI's tasks Ghosh said that "the transition to socialism by parliamentary path cannot be envisaged except through immediate and constant struggle for the defence and enlargement of democratic liberties."[34]

The documents of the Palghat Congress (Report of the Central Committee and the Political Resolution) were an application of the peaceful transition thesis to India. The long-term objective of a government of people's democracy remained but the immediate aim was to "progressively dislodge the bourgeoisie from its dominant position in the national government." The tactics worked out by the resolution required support to every government measure "against imperialism and feudalism" but resistance to policies which helped imperialism, feudalism, and the monopolies, drawing the mass of Congressmen into it. There was to be no "general united front" with Congress but the democratic front did not mean an anti-Congress front either.[35] In sum, the Palghat documents initiated action for peaceful transition by seeking to rally the leftist forces around the CPI, mobilizing the masses, sharpen class struggle and use the left wing in the Congress Party to force a left-ward shift in its policies.

The CPI right-wing was not reconciled to its defeat at Palghat. It sought to reopen the debate on the basis of a Soviet article which said the Nehru Government had embarked on non-capitalist development, that is towards social-

---

[34] "The Report of Comrade Ajoy Ghosh to the Fourth Congress of CPI on XX Congress of the CPSU" (unpublished document).
[35] "Political Resolution," New Age, 20 May 1956.

ism through a growing role for state sector.[36] Through
this article, the Soviet leadership was perhaps trying to bring
the CPI closer to Nehru. But the Central Committee rejected the understanding behind the article and the centrists
held their ground.

The CPI went into the 1957 election battle on the basis
of its understanding at Palghat. The strategy of peaceful
transition seemed to have paid off in Kerala where the party
won power. The ministry there, led by the CPI, became an
important factor in the country's political life. The Congress
had lost heavily but the right, and not the left, was the bene-
ficiary.

Shortly thereafter, a CPI delegation led by Ghosh participated in the Moscow (November 1957) meeting of communist parties where the Chinese attacked Soviet thesis of
peaceful transition and forced its modification. The CPI,
which was quick to implement the Soviet strategy, also came
under heavy attack especially for its decision to form a ministry in Kerala. A latter-day Chinese commentary was to
denounce the communist-led ministry as "the infamous
model of peaceful transition and 'parliamentary road' which
had won praise from both U.S. imperialists and modern
revisionists."[37]

Thereafter CPI decided to hold an extraordinary congress
to assess the changed situation. The growing strength of
the rightist forces inside and outside the Congress seemed
to worry the party most. The Congress was in crisis and the
government's planning and economic policies had run into
a crisis and were coming under rightist attack. United States

[36] Modeste Rubinstein, "A Non-Capitalist Path for Under-
developed Countries," New Times, July 1956 and August 1956.
[37] "Parliamentary Road in India—A Fiasco," Peking Review, 31
January 1969.

pressure on India was also mounting. So the extreme right had to be fought. The reactionaries outside the Congress who were out to scuttle the Second Five Year Plan had no popular mass base but derived their strength from similar elements in the Congress and from some of the government policies. So it had to be a simultaneous battle against the right wing reaction and the "anti-people" government policies.[38] The rightists wanted a Congress-Communist coalition to counter the reactionary trends and mounting United States pressure on India. But the Congress attempts to dislodge the Kerala ministry inhibited them from doing so.

The most significant development at Amritsar was the formal proclamation of CPI's resolve to achieve peaceful transition to socialism. The new party constitution incorporated this in its preamble and it was an unqualified commitment. Ghosh later explained that "peaceful methods for us are neither a creed nor a tactic. It is a policy—a seriously meant policy."[39]

Beginning with 1950, there had been no let up in Soviet pressure on the CPI. As soon as Moscow decided to stop its cold war against Nehru, it tried to get the CPI to call off the Telengana armed struggle. The CPI had adopted a new programme and tactical line 1951 with Soviet approval. The tactical line provided for armed struggle but that was not to be part of immediate programme. Once the CPI had called off the Telengana insurrection, it was easy for the Soviet leadership to persuade it to settle for parliamentarism in 1952, and for peaceful transition in 1957. The CPI became a pressure group and a lobby for the Soviet

---

[38] *Resolutions of the Communist Party of India*, Communist Party of India, New Delhi, 1958, p. 10.
[39] *New Age*, 18 May 1958.

Union in a cold war situation. It was in the Soviet interest
later to extend economic aid to India and to direct the CPI
to support Nehru's policies because India's neutral position
was a useful lever for the Soviet Union in the cold war.

Concept of National Democracy

For the CPI it was an excruciating interlude between its
Fifth and Sixth Congresses (1958-61). In mid-1959, the
Communist-led ministry in Kerala was dismissed by Nehru
through a constitutional coup engineered by his party headed
by Indira Gandhi. The CPI, formally committed to peaceful transition, found its hopes of winning power in other
States through elections belied. In the re-elections in Kerala
the party was routed. The Sino-Soviet ideological dispute
broke out in the open and the Sino-Indian border dispute
was building up into an armed confrontation. An interaction of the two disputes aggravated an already complex
situation in the CPI taking it to the verge of a split at its
Sixth Congress. The interlude revealed divergent Soviet and
Chinese assessments of the Indian bourgeoisie and the
potential of the Indian revolution. The deterioration in
Sino-Indian relations was accompanied by growing Soviet
solicitude for Nehru and his government and even implied
diplomatic support to India against China. On 9 September
1959, the Soviet Union declared the neutrality in the Sino-
Indian border dispute.[40] The Chinese were to describe this
"diplomatic rocket" as the first overt disclosure of Sino-
Soviet differences.[41] The Soviet leadership, charmed by the

[40] *Pravda*, 10 September 1959.
[41] "No One Can Save the Indian Reactionaries From Their
Political Bankruptcy," *People's Daily*, 22 August 1963; *Peking
Review*, 30 August 1963.

economic achievements of the Indian bourgeoisie, ignored Chinese charges of Indian interference in Tibet, maintained studied silence on the Kerala coup, and extended massive industrial credit to the Nehru Government within a month of the coup. The Chinese, who had been reassessing Nehru and the Indian bourgeoisie in early 1959, noticed in 1960 not only monopolistic characteristics in the Indian bourgeoisie but also collusion with foreign imperialists.

The CPI was caught in the Moscow-Peking cross fire. Already deadlocked over the strategy and tactics of revolution and divided over the Sino-Indian border dispute, it was being drawn into the vortex of the Sino-Soviet ideological dispute. By declaring neutrality in the Sino-Indian border dispute the Soviet Union relieved domestic pressure on the CPI and strengthened the dominant right faction which was supporting Nehru's policies. In return this faction committed the party to Soviet positions in the ideological dispute. Its resolution held that Sino-Indian border dispute was not just an issue between the two countries. The CPC's new assessment of the role of India's national bourgeoisie had found its "sharpest and most devastating expression" on this issue and the Chinese assessment was central to the understanding of the 12-party Moscow declaration of 1957. The resolution condemned the Chinese party and endorsed Soviet positions on non-inevitability of war, peaceful transition, and national liberation movement.[42]

This was a few weeks before the Moscow conference of world communist parties in November 1960 claimed by the CPI the result of its initiative.[43] The preparatory commis-

[42] "On Certain Questions Before the International Communist Movement," Resolution of the Central Executive Committee of the CPI, September 1960, unabridged version (unpublished document).
[43] Link, 30 October 1960.

sion for the conference included India's Ajoy Ghosh and its
work was based on a secret 84-page CPSU letter on the ideological dispute to some of the fraternal parties on the ideological dispute, the 160-page CPC rejoinder to it, and,
significantly, the CPI Central Executive's resolution (afore-
mentioned) on the dispute. The 81-party Moscow statement included a new formulation—the national democratic
state, described as a form of transition to socialism in developing countries, especially in the nonaligned countries of
the peace zone where the national bourgeoisie played an
objectively progressive role and deserved political and economic aid. The national democratic state was one that had
won complete economic independence from imperialism and
was ruled by a broad anti-imperialist front including the
national bourgeoisie, the peasantry, and the proletariat. The
working class was to evolve as its leader only gradually.

The concept of national democracy is an innovation of
Soviet-Indian revisionism. It was at once justification of
Soviet aid to India and some other Asian countries whose
bourgeoisie the Soviets considered objectively progressive,
and a corollary to the concept of peaceful transition. Mohit
Sen, a CPI theoretician, claimed that though "the state of
national democracy" was a new concept in the international
communist movement, his party has been since 1956 putting forward a programme and producing an analysis which
was the same as the Moscow statement's. It was the culmi-
nation of a very precise formulation of the CPI.[44] Ajoy
Ghosh, who had outlined a programme for a "national democratic front" in India as early as February 1956 (on the eve
of the 20th CPSU Congress) and had anticipated the Soviet
thesis of peaceful coexistence, was among those who pre-

[44] Maral (monthly), New Delhi, January 1961.

pared the documents for the Moscow conference. So the CPI can legitimately claim the concept of national democracy as its contribution to the international communist movement.

The Chinese attitude to Soviet aid to countries outside the socialist bloc precluded support to this concept. There was a veiled CPC attack on it on the eve of the 22nd CPSU Congress.[45] The nature of the obligations of an advanced communist world to the emerging communist world has been one of the issues in the Sino-Soviet conflict and the CPC has thought Soviet aid to China has been niggardly and the Soviet leadership equated communist countries with developing non-Western countries like India in the matter of aid. The Soviet leadership pursued its national interests and sought a big power alliance with U.S. imperialism to gain world domination. The CPC was to develop this theme later in its polemics with the CPSU but certainly the concept of a national democratic state, to the extent it implied justification of Soviet aid to the bourgeoisie of countries like India, was an irritant in the Sino-Soviet relations.

This controversial concept gave a new dimension to the CPI's continuing struggle for a new programme amidst an alarming right-ward shift in the government's policies and growing strength of the right forces. Central to the debate was the attitude to the ruling Congress Party and the character of the bourgeoisie but it took a predictable form: national democracy versus people's democracy. Ghosh and the right which backed him advocated the goal of national democratic government through a national democratic front while the left wanted an altogether narrower front than what Ghosh had in view and the goal was to be people's demo-

[45] *People's Daily*, 10 October 1961.

cracy. The right thought that India's bourgeois democracy could metamarphose into a national democracy and placed heavy reliance on Soviet aid as the instrument to secure it. The left thought the bourgeoisie was compromising with domestic reaction and imperialism, and Soviet aid though necessary was being used by the bourgeoisie as a bargaining counter for more aid from the West. The front proposed by the right was to be a four-class alliance and the national bourgeoisie which might not join it in the first instance could be drawn in as the reactionary offensive grew and people stepped up pressure. The emphasis here was on the inclusion of Congressmen and at least a section of their leadership. The right was minimizing and even ignoring the compromising role of the national bourgeoisie. The left was to point out later[46] that the Moscow statement had also underscored the fact that the national bourgeoisie tended to compromise with imperialism and domestic reaction and contradictions developed.

At the Sixth Congress in Vijayawada early in 1961, the right and the left were poised for a showdown but the high-powered CPSU delegation intervened to salvage the rightist line. Mikhail Suslov, Secretary of the Central Committee, who was leading the delegation (first-ever to a CPI congress) through his round about and involute refutation of the leftist line,[47] helped the right offensive against the left. His observation that India had taken the road of "sovereign independent development" and had become independent "for ever" was an attack on the leftist formulation that India was an appendage of the United States. He suggested that India's national bourgeoisie was a dependable, patriotic force

[46] *Fight Against Revisionism*, Communist Party of India (M), 1966, p. 8.
[47] "Suslov Greets Our Party Congress," *New Age*, 23 April 1961.

when he referred to the CPI's struggle "had in hand with the country's other patriotic forces for elimination of economic backwardness, building up a stable and independent economy." This swung the balance in favour of the rightists and saved their programme draft from defeat and averted an open split. The congress shelved the question of programme but could not put off the political resolution dealing with immediate tasks. Ghosh's compromise line prevailed over the right and left drafts and in its amended, final form represented a limited victory for the left. It rejected the rightist line of a general united front with the Congress but advocated the tactic of unity with struggle. The slogan of power was a government of national democracy or a government of the national democratic front. The issue of national democracy versus people's democracy raised in the rival programme drafts remained unresolved. It was a compromise "centrist" position. The resolution called for a struggle to defeat the reaction and to force a policy shift to the left and a new correlation of forces.[48] The government of national democracy was to be an instrument of struggle against reactionary forces and for carrying forward the non-capitalist path. The left might have succeeded in blocking a shift to the right (towards a general united front with the Congress) but the political resolution was an opportunist compromise to prevent a split. It preserved intact all the central elements of the rightist line including reliance on non-capitalist development. The differences remained unresolved and the logic of the compromise was the open split in 1964.

[48] New Age, 7 May 1961. Also as pamphlet, National Democratic Front for National Democratic Tasks, Communist Party of India, New Delhi, 1961.

Soviet Aid, the Irritant

Shortly after the CPI's Vijayawada Congress, the Sino-Soviet ideological dispute took the form of an open confrontation at the 22nd CPSU Congress. Khrushchev's attacks on Albania and his denigration of Stalin touched off a storm of anti-Soviet protests from several State units of the CPI. Late in 1961, Sino-Indian relations became strained over the border dispute, each side charging the other with intrusions. This had its impact on the CPI and Ghosh was obliged to charge China with intrusions[49] and in the process invite a blistering *People's Daily* attack which charged Nehru with whipping up a "hate China" campaign to bolster the election chances of his party, and Ghosh with "trailing behind" Nehru.[50]

Ghosh died on the eve of the general elections early in 1962. The growing tension on the Sino-Indian border added to the CPI's differences over its attitude to the Nehru government. When the dispute escalated into a military conflict in October-November 1962, the CPI branded China aggressor and the difference here was limited to the question of "imperialist military aid" India was getting to fight China. Soviet Union, after initial neutrality, moved closer to the Indian position, largely due to the CPI's lobbying on behalf of the Nehru Government. There was a general intensification of the Sino-Soviet polemics during December 1962-March 1963.

Amidst the border war came a fresh CPC assessment of Nehru, charging India with aggression against China and tracing the alleged Indian belligerence to the class nature of

[49] *New Age*, 26 November 1961.
[50] *People's Daily*, 7 November 1961.

its ruling alliance whose interests were linked with those of imperialists. In sum it said Nehru had "thrown away the banner of opposition to imperialism" and had "suited himself" to the needs of United States imperialism becoming its "busy spokesman." Bourgeois nationalism under different conditions played different historical roles. Nehru "who once represented, to a certain degree, the interests of the Indian national bourgeoisie ... became a loyal representative of the big bourgeois and big landlords of India." When contradictions between imperialism and the Indian nation sharpened, the Nehru Government, under the pressure of the masses, showed a certain degree of difference from imperialism. But the class nature of the big bourgeoisie and the landlords determined that Nehru depend on imperialism and serve it more and more. The article referred to the dominance of foreign capital in India's economy after independence and the growing dependence of the Indian government and foreign aid.

On foreign policy, it said that at one stage, Nehru's role had helped world peace (e.g. his refusal to join military blocs, denial of bases to imperialists, declaration of non-alignment and *Panchsheel,* and his positive role in sponsoring the Afro-Asian conference). Nevertheless it was subservient to imperialism because Nehru was criticizing imperialism "in a small way" but was "helping it in a big way." The United States wanted to convert India into its market for both commodities and capital and therefore had shifted its attitude to Nehru's "nonalignment." From refusal to supply the Indian big bourgeoisie machineral and know-how, it was now keen on cooperation with it for joint exploitation of the Indian people. "In a word, U.S. imperialism pursues a policy of paying a high price to buy over the

Indian big bourgeoisie represented by Nehru."[51]

The CPC regarded India nonaligned until the end of the Bandung phase (1955-1959). The Afro-Asian confe-rence in Bandung (April 1955) represented perhaps the peak of Sino-Indian amity. The Soviet diplomatic offensive in South-East Asia (the visit of Khurshchev and Bulganian to India, Indonesia, and Afghanistan) began after Bandung and the Sino-Indian relations began to deteriorate in direct proportion to the growth of Sino-Soviet relations.

The Sino-Indian border flare-up in 1962 was in a sense the function of the Sino-Soviet ideological dispute. In an-other sense, India itself was a factor in the dispute.

A confidential CPSU letter to parties of the "socialist" camp, in reply to a confidential CPC memo to 11 ruling parties charging India with aggression, throws new light on Soviet attitude to the Sino-Indian border dispute. Accord-ing to the CPSU, China invaded India without informing Soviet Union which had repeatedly offered to mediate in the dispute. India was willing to negotiate but China began talks merely to gain time for "aggressive" actions putting Soviet Union in a "difficult position." The letter blamed China for forcing India into dependence on Western mili-tary aid. Sino-Indian friendship, built over years and strengthened by treaties and economic aid, was brought un-der strain. The Soviet Union had been supplying Indian "means of self-defence" and this represented "a tremondous victory over the United States and England."

The letter reveals that China sought Soviet aid "in the invasion which it had itself provoked." The Soviet Union begged the Chinese to stop the military operations forth-

---

[51] "More on Nehru's Philosophy in the Light of the Sino-Indian Boundary Question," *People's Daily*, 27 October 1962.

with and offered to mediate. Soviet Union wanted to prevent India from turning to the United States and Great Britain for military aid.

The Soviet Union, the letter also reveals, had stopped all deliveries of military material to India during the Sino-Indian border conflict. Only after the conflict had ended did the Soviet Union come to the conclusion that "there was no ground for not fulfilling its commitments" to India.[52]

As the Sino-Soviet ideological dispute intensified early in 1963, third parties were forced to take sides. The CPI attacked the Chinese ideological positions,[53] besides charging the CPC was violating the 1957 Moscow declaration and the 1960 Moscow statement. The CPC reply came in the form of the famous People's Daily article "Mirror For Revisionists"[54] which compared Dange to Tito, as providing the second mirror for revisionists. The CPI, like the Yugoslav party, was the litmus test of Marxism-Leninism.

Before Dange could reply to the Peking attack,[55] a Red Flag commentator denounced Nehru's socialist pattern as nothing but a capitalist society. "Some revisionists in India" had been asking people to rally around Nehru without reservations.[56]

The CPC has since reserved its sharpest criticism for

<hr>

[52] Excerpts from the letter are reproduced in David Floyd, Mao Against Khrushchev, Pall Mall, London, 1964.
[53] "On Certain Questions Affecting the Unity of the International Communist Movement," CPI National Council Resolution, New Age, 17 February 1963.
[54] People's Daily, 9 March 1963.
[55] "Neither Revisionism nor Dogmatism is Our Guide," New Age, 21 April 1963.
[56] "What Kind of Stuff is Nehru's Much Advertised Socialism?" Red Flag, 1 April 1963.

Soviet economic and military aid to India. The military pressure on the Indian border was part of the Chinese effort to force a change in Soviet policies towards India, when other efforts had failed. This in turn widened Sino-Soviet differences over India, the Soviet Union charging China with forcing India into turning to the West for military aid. In the process, China had succeeded in establishing that India was no longer nonaligned and was accepting military aid from the West and Soviet arms aid and diplomatic aid to India was untenable by socialist norms.

The CPC had to make India the touchstone of Soviet bona fides about world revolution. The Soviet argument that its support to the national bourgeoisie of developing countries like India was a legitimate, albeit temporary expedient as long as it helped colonial liberation was not accepted by the CPC. As early as October 1963, the CPC had outlined its thesis on which Lin's Third World Strategy was based. Briefly it was: various types of contradictions in the world were concentrated in vast areas of the Third World which were storm centres of revolution; the national democratic revolutionary movement in these areas and the international socialist revolutionary movement were the two great historic currents of the time; the national democratic revolution in these areas were an important component of the contemporary world revolution; the anti-imperialist struggle in the Third World was undermining foundations of imperialism and colonialism and therefore a mighty force for peace; in a sense the whole cause of the international proletarian revolution hinged on the outcome of these struggles; and, therefore, the anti-imperialist struggle in the Third World was definitely not merely of regional significance but was one of overall importance to the whole cause of proletarian revolution.[57]

By implementing the Third World strategy in mid-1967, the CPC was escalating its ideological dispute with the CPSU to a higher plane by challenging the Soviet general line. Since in the Chinese view the CPSU had made India the show case of revisionist concepts like "national democracy" and "peaceful transition" and was commending the model to Burma and Indonesia among other countries, the CPC felt the need for a radical reassertion of the Chinese model of revolution for the Third World. India was central to Lin's Third World strategy and just as the CPSU had to prove that non-capitalist development and peaceful transition was possible in India, the CPC had to prove that neither of these were possible and India's path to revolution lay in an agrarian revolution through a Maoist people's war.

[57] "Apologists of Neo-colonialism," Peking Review, 25 October 1963.

CHAPTER TWO

THE ROAD TO
NAXALBARI

A MINUSCULE PEASANT revolt in Naxalbari, a 270-square mile
enclave of 80,000 people, provided the Communist Party of
China in mid-1967 not only an opportunity to implement
the strategy of transferring its struggle against the United
States and the Soviet revisionists to the Third World activa-
ting and intensifying the national liberation movement but
also an occasion for a fundamental evaluation of the Indian
revolution and to spell out the Maoist line for India. Naxalbari was just another prosaic village, a microcosm of semi-
feudal India, until the uprising in March 1967. It came
to be vested with certain symbolism by Indian Maoists who
saw in it elements of the famous 1926-27 Hunan peasant
uprising in China.

An authoritative CPC article, poetically titled "Spring
Thunder Over India" saw in Naxalbari the emergence of a
"red area of revolutionary armed struggle." It went ahead
to provide guidance, both in theory and practice, to the revolutionary groups of the Communist Party of India (Marxist) whose weakness for the parliamentary path had disap-
pointed the CPC. It laid down the broad strategy for India's
"people's war" against the four "big mountains"—"imperialism, Soviet revisionism, feudalism and bureaucrat-capital-
ism."[1]

[1] "Spring Thunder Over India," *People's Daily*, 5 July 1967.

India was only "nominally independent, in fact nothing more than a semi-colonial, semi-feudal country." Its revolution must rely on the peasants, establish base areas in the countryside and use the countryside to encircle the cities. As Mao had said the peasants constituted the main force in the national democratic revolution and were the most reliable and numerous allies of the proletariat. By integrating itself with the peasantry, the proletariat would be able to bring about "earth-shaking changes in the vast countryside and defeat any powerful enemy in a soul stirring people's war."

The specific feature of the Indian revolution, like that of the Chinese revolution, was armed revolution fighting armed counter-revolution. Armed struggle was the only road for India, the article declared. More specifically, it meant arousing the peasant masses to "deal blows at the armed suppression of imperialists and reactionaries, who are temporarily stronger than the revolutionary forces, but using the whole set of flexible strategy and tactics of people's war personally worked out by Chairman Mao, and to persist in protracted armed struggle and seize victory of the revolution step by step."[2]

Revolutionary rural bases was to be the king-pin of the strategy and the Indian countryside, where the reactionary rule was weak, provided the broad areas in which the revolutionaries "can manoeuvre freely." One advanced base area after another, from isolated points into a vast expanse, from small areas into extensive ones, and an expansion in a series of waves, and in the process a people's army of a new type—the specifics were familiar.

In June-July 1967, with Naxalbari the CPC regarded the Indian situation opportune for a protracted people's war but

[2] Ibid.

the road to Naxalbari was a long one. Shortly after the victory of the Chinese revolution, a programme for united action of the communist parties of Asia was outlined by Liu Shao-chi on behalf of the CPC.[3] The Chinese revolution was held out as the model for the rest of Asia but the Indian communists who were engaged in a peasant armed struggle in Telengana were cautioned against launching an immediate people's war. An authoritative CPC article[4] had commended Liu's line which had been endorsed by the Cominform[5] but hastened to suggest that Communist Party of India's enthusiasm here was misplaced. Recalling that General Secretary B. T. Ranadive had hailed the Cominform statement and declared his "full acceptance" of its conclusions, the article observed that while armed struggle against imperialism was necessary for colonial liberation, "the time and place for conducting this kind of revolutionary armed struggle must be decided according to concrete conditions. It can by no means be conducted in any colony or any semi-colony at any time without necessary conditions or precautions." Where objective conditions permitted armed struggle, victory still depended on subjective conditions like whether the people had a working class party and the proper leadership or not.

It was not until after Naxalbari that the CPC had suggested even remotely that India was ready for people's war or saw the objective conditions for it. Contrary to the

[3] "Speech by Liu Shao-chi at the Conference of Trade Unions of Asia and Oceania," For a Lasting Peace, For a People's Democracy, 30 December 1949.
[4] "Armed People Opposes Armed Counter-revolution," People's Daily, 16 June 1950, People's China, 1 July 1950.
[5] "Mighty Advance of the National Liberation Movement in Colonies and Semi-Colonies," For a Lasting Peace for a People's Democracy, 27 January 1950.

general belief, the split in the CPI in 1964 was not the result of a Moscow-Peking polarization as part of the international communist schism. The origins of the Indian communist split predate both the Sino-Soviet ideological dispute and the Sino-Indian border dispute though these factors interacted on an existing pattern of differences over the programme and tactical line. The international schism ruled out any mediation by the CPSU or CPC and the split became open. While the post-split Communist Party of India had committed itself to Soviet positions in the ideological dispute the breakaway section that later became the majority Communist Party of India (Marxist) had left the ideological issue open at its foundation congress in 1964. While the CPI had accepted the Soviet thesis of peaceful transition and the concept of national democracy, the CPI (M) had equivocated on peaceful transition while rejecting the concept of national democracy. It has placed the onus of peaceful transition on the ruling classes. Its programme had declared:

By developing a powerful mass revolutionary movement, by combining parliamentary and extra-parliamentary forms of struggle, the working class and its allies will try their utmost to overcome the resistance of the forces of reaction and to bring about these transformations through peaceful means.

However, it needed always to be borne in mind that the ruling classes never relinquish their power voluntarily. They seek to defy the will of the people and seek to reverse it by lawlessness and violence. It is therefore, necessary for the revolutionary forces to be vigilant and so orientate their work that they can face up to all contingencies, to any twist and turn in the political life of the country.[6]

The CPC was very cautious in its attitude to the new party in India though it had no doubt about the "revisionist" character of the old party (pro-Soviet Communist Party of India). The new party had held its foundation congress in October-November 1964, but there was no reference to the party in the Chinese mass media until after the round up of its leaders which began on 30 December 1964. *People's Daily* of 17 January condemned the arrest (of 800 functionaries including Politbureau members) as "another counter-revolutionary action" of the Indian government to suppress the national democratic movement. . "The big bourgeoisie and the big landlord class of India and the imperialists and modern revisionists were alarmed beyond measure" at the holding of the CPI(M)'s congress and the "great success achieved by it."

Voicing the "deep indignation" of Chinese people at the arrests, the *People's Daily* hoped the CPI (M)'s ranks will swell and it would prove to the "genuine" representative of the Indian people and their nation, "uphold truth and adhere to Marxism-Leninism and proletarian internationalism."[7]

A few weeks later, the CPC denounced the "Consultative Meeting of the Communist and Workers' Parties" called in Moscow by the new CPSU leadership as "schismatic" and attacked the CPI for attending it. The CPI (M), which had opposed the meeting, was praised for its stand and

[6] *Programme of the Communist Party of India (M)*, Calcutta, 1965.

[7] Commentator, "Another Glaring Exposure of the Indian Government's Reactionary Features," *People's Daily*, 17 January 1965.

bracketed with the other "genuine" communist parties, which had taken a similar stand, viz. of Albania, Indonesia, Japan, Korea, and Rumania.[8]

India's "Double Alignment"

During the year, Chinese attacks on India were limited to foreign policy issues, aimed at proving India's double-alignment with the United States and Soviet Union and complicity in the big power game to contain China. When Prime Minister Lal Bahadur Shastri visited Soviet Union in May, *People's Daily* wrote a comprehensive attack on India's foreign policy but made no reference to the domestic situation. India was charged with receiving a large amount of United States military aid and an air umbrella, with providing United States air and naval bases, with "acting as a U.S. accomplice" in Congo (Leopoldville), Cyprus, Dominican Republic, and on the Malaysian question. It was not at all surprising that the United States should be appreciating Shastri's role on Vietnam, the article said. "But on what grounds," it asked, "did the Soviet leaders allege that this favourite of Washington's 'restrains the forces of war and strengthens the forces of peace'?" The Soviet leaders were asking Shastri to make a "new, worthy contribution" to solving the Vietnam problem. The reason: Shastri was a "rare anti-China cavaliar" and "Washington's pet." The Soviet leadership's alignment with the "Indian reactionaries" against China was an "integral part" of Khrushchevian revisionism. The "Indian reactionaries" were "political duds" and it was futile to "whitewash them politically or to give

[8] NCNA, 22 March 1965.

them an economic shot in the arm."[9]

In August, the CPC denounced Shastri-Tito communique from Belgrade which covered the Vietnam issue:

> ... more and more aligned countries have come to see clearly that the only way to settle the Vietnam question is by the withdrawal of American troops from south Vietnam. They have also come to see that the Tito group and the Indian reactionaries are nothing but American agents.[10]

Burma's Ne Win was still the model nonaligned leader meriting a "warm welcome."[11]

The Soviet stand on the Sino-Indian border dispute and continued Soviet economic and military aid to India invited steady Chinese attacks which tended to emphasize the convergence of United States and Soviet interests in India. "By receiving 'military' aid from the Soviet Union, the Indian government hopes to conceal its alliance with Washington, claiming that between the two it is 'nonaligned' and 'neutral'," said an article. Military aid from United States and Soviet Union to India were of the "same nature" aimed against China and helping war preparations, which threatened India's neighbours and peace.[12]

Chinese reaction to the Indo-Pakistani war (September-October) was predictable. Premier Chou En-lai condemned "India's aggression" as "a threat to Asian peace" and

[9] Observer, "What Shastri's Soviet Trip Reveals," *People's Daily*, 27 May 1965; *Peking Review*, 4 June 1965.

[10] Observer, "Poor Salesman for an American Plot," *People's Daily*, 9 August 1965; *Peking Review*, 13 August 1965.

[11] *Peking Review*, 30 July 1965.

[12] Shish Yen, "'Non-aligned' India's Double Alignment," *Peking Review*, 13 August 1965.

saw "consent and support" of the United States, and
encouragements of the modern "revisionists" to the "military
adventure."[13] A *People's Daily* editorial supported Pakistan's
"just struggle against aggression" and the Kashmir people's
"struggle for national self-determination."[14]   United States
hoped to cut Pakistan down to size because it could not
bear the latter's "independent" policies, the Soviet leadership
pretended to be impartial but actually favoured Indian
reactionaries and was "not one whit inferior" to United
States imperialists. The Soviet leadership tried to cover up
Indian aggression, to defend its "bankrupt nonalignment"
by describing its policy as one of "peace and peaceful coexistence."[15]

The foreign policy debate had begun inside the CPC and
Lin Piao had proposed his Third World strategy. While
attacks on Soviet "betrayal" of the national liberation movement and the "united action" move in Vietnam continued
there was no serious effort to activate the movement itself.
The CPC observed the fifth anniversary of the 1960 Moscow
statement charging the Communist Party of Soviet Union
with betraying both 1957 declaration and the 1960 statement
by pressing forward the "anti-revolutionary line" of peaceful
coexistence, peaceful competition, and peaceful transition.
"They themselves do not want revolution and forbid others
to make revolution."[16]

But a document of the Peruvian Communist Party, published approvingly by the CPC, incorporated all the ingredi-

13 *Peking Review*, 17 September 1965.
14 "Indian Reactionaries are the Out-and-out Aggressors," *People's
Daily*, 11 September 1965.
15 "Who Backs the Indian Aggressor?" *People's Daily*, 10 Sep
tember, 1965; *Peking Review*, 24 September 1965.
16 Editorial Department of *People's Daily*, *Peking Review*, 1
January 1966.

cnts of the Lin line. Reporting the beginning of armed
struggle in Peru, it said the political situation confronting
the Peruvian people was one developing within the framework of an international situation. That was favourable to
the national liberation struggle of oppressed people against
United States imperialism and its "stooges." Asia, Africa, and
Latin America had become the focal point of the fundamental
contradictions in the world and were the weakest sectors of
the imperialist colonial empire. The contradiction between the
oppressed nations and imperialism was the most acute and
major one. The contradictions centring on Vietnam were
being successfully resolved through armed struggle and the
Vietnam war proved that United States imperialism, however powerful can be defeated because, as Mao had said, the
outcome of a war was decided not by weapons but by man.[17]

Underscoring a world-wide united front against United
States the Peruvian party said the centre of Marxism-Leninism had shifted from Europe to Asia, from Soviet Union to
China. The life and death struggle against imperialism and
world reaction led by the Chinese party was proof of this.[18]

The CPC media also made a passing reference to the
armed struggle which had been developing in Thailand
since 1961.[19] The changing Indian situation (as a result of
two successive drought years and the resulting economic
recession) did not go unnoticed by the CPC. An article
said that faced with an acute food shortage, Indian politi-
cians were arguing about who to blame—failure of monsoons
or failure of policy—and were "placing their main hopes on

[17] "Political Report and Resolution of the Peruvian C.P.," Peking
Review, 7 January 1966.
[18] "Fifth National Conference of the Peruvian Communist Party,"
Peking Review, 28 March 1966.
[19] "Facts on File," Peking Review, 4 March 1966.

hand-outs from their Washington masters." And Washington was not missing the chance to exploit India's food difficulties and tighten its own control over the country. The article reported a widespread "anti-hunger struggle" and rumblings of a revolt in the countryside. Hard-pressed peasants were fighting landlords and police and class contradictions and class struggle were becoming sharp in urban and rural areas. Though land reforms were promised at the time of Independence, 1947, the Indian government representing the big bourgeoisie and big landlord interests had not changed the system of land ownership. Since 1962 (Sino-Indian border war), there was not even the talk of land reforms,[20] it said.

A more direct attack on the Indian government's policies was to come at the Afro-Asian Writers' Emergency Meeting in Peking two months later. A resolution supported the "growing militant struggle" against the "big bourgeois-landlord" government of India which had "not only mortgaged India's economy, independence and sovereignty to imperialists, but has also betrayed the historic principles of Afro-Asian solidarity" adopted at the Bandung conference, 1955. It had allied itself with the "most reactionary regimes in Asia," e.g. of Japan, Taiwan, Malaysia, and Indonesia, to serve the United States strategy of world domination. Donning the "fraudulent, tattered grab of nonalignment, and colluding with the Dange clique, [pro-Moscow Communist Party of India], the traitors to the national working class and socialism, it has been shamelessly acting as the paid agents of U.S. imperialism and its cat's paw for the suppression and domination of the people's of Asia and Africa and the

---

[20] Ting Chuan, "Food Crisis and Why," *Peking Review*, 11 March 1966.

U.S. plans of aggression against the People's Republic of China, the bulwark of world revolutionary movements and staunch defender of peace."

The CPC commemorated the first anniversary of Lin's thesis with the declaration that "revolutionary military strategy of people's war, created by Mao Tse-tung, is the only correct and victorious strategy for the oppressed people to defeat all enemies."[21] The general attack continued to be on the "unity in action" line.

Support to "Class Struggle"

A few months before the fourth general elections, scheduled for February 1967, there was a general deterioration of law and order alongside a serious economic crisis. The extreme right-wing Hindu revivalist forces made cow slaughter ban an election issue and campaigned massively for it in northern India. There was also a wave of student unrest and strike action by government employees in several States. The CPC saw in this a "sharpening of class contradictions," "the inevitable outcome of the reactionary policies" of the government at home and its kow-towing to United States and Soviet Union abroad. A *Peking Review* article saw in the famous cow protection march on Parliament House in New Delhi (which ended in police shooting) an explosion of the anger against the government, part of the "violent storm of popular opposition sweeping the country." The national economy had been pushed to the brink of bankrup-

---

[21] Tung Ming, "The People's Revolutionary Strategy Will Surely Triumph Over U.S. Imperialism's Counter-Revolution Strategy," *Peking Review*, 9 September 1966.

tcy and the people plunged into deep misery.[22]

A commentary on the student unrest said that the Indian students movement, mainly for educational reforms and scaling down of fees, had quickly turned into a "fierce political struggle" answering the "bloody suppression" with violence. It was part of the "hightide of the Indian people's struggle," reflecting the sharpened class contradictions.[23]

India approached its general elections amidst turmoil and serious doubts about the possibility of a peaceful and orderly poll. The CPI (M), which in the Chinese view was India's only genuine communist party (in the Soviet view, it was the CPI), worked out its election strategy in June 1966. The main objective was breaking the Congress Party's power monopoly and formation of alternative governments wherever possible; defeating the Congress in as many constituencies as possible; and increasing the CPI (M)'s representation and strengthening democratic opposition in the federal Parliament and State legislatures. In September, its Politbureau asked the State committees to decide finally the seats the party would contest on the basis of its influence and organizational strength; and generally develop mass movements and consolidate political influence.[24]

The CPI (M)'s programme had equivocated on the question of peaceful transition and its enthusiasm for the parliamentary system, as evident from its election tactics, was to be expected. Despite its accent on the need to fight both "imperialism and revisionism," in actual practice its differ-

[22] "Indian People Rise up in Resistance," Peking Review, 16 November 1966.
[23] "Student Movement in India," Peking Review, 2 December 1966.
[24] "Election Review and Party's Tasks," Communist Party of India (Marxist), Calcutta, 1967, pp. 9-10.

ences with the CPI had become minimal as long as both
were participating in the parliamentary system. At least, this
seemed to be the Chinese reading by the end of 1966.

On the eve of the elections, there was gushing optimism
in the CPC's reading of the revolutionary situation. India
had been swept by a series of "stormy struggles" during 1966
which continued in full flood in the new year, "making a
violent assault on the rule of Indian reactionaries." The
accent was on working class action. "The Indian workers
are the main force in the struggle." Students also took an
active part but the struggle, hitherto confined to cities, was
spreading to the villages. People were realizing that the root
cause of their misery lay in the government which represented the interests of the big bourgeoisie and big landlords. Its
overthrow was absolutely essential. Economic and political
struggles were coming together to reinforce each other. In
the second half of 1966, anti-suppression and anti-tyranny
had become the general slogans of the demonstrators who
had also demanded the exit of the Congress government
propped by United States imperialism and Soviet revisionism. The review also referred to the revolts of ethnic minorities and mentioned the Mizo revolt in Assam.[25]

The elections ended in a shattering defeat for the Congress Party, which lost office in eight of the 17 States and
returned to power with a shrunken majority in the federal
Parliament. Its vote dropped from 44.72 per cent in 1962 to
37.87 per cent in 1967, and its strength in Parliament, from
358 to 282, that is from 70 per cent to 55 per cent. In
Kerala, the CPI (M)-led alliance swept to power and in
West Bengal, a CPI (M)-led front together with another

_____

[25] "India: Anti-Tyranny Struggles Rock Reactionary Rule,"
Peking Review, 24 February 1967.

front in which the CPI was a partner, came to power. Thus the CPI(M) was the dominant partner in two State governments.

It took nearly a month for the CPC to react to the post-election situation. Back in power with a reduced majority at the federal level, the Congress government was "more reactionary than ever and still more subservient to Soviet revisionism." The Congress party, a tool of the ruling classes for 20 years, "has now become ineffective in face of the people's resistance."

The impressive gains of the rightist parties did not go unnoticed. The Swatantra Party (representing the "comprador bourgeoisie") had emerged the second largest force in Parliament and had won power in Orissa. Jan Sangh (representing "feudal and religious forces") had become the third party and gained control of Delhi, the capital. Over a hundred feudal lords and aristocrats had got into Parliament and there was a chance of feudal leaders becoming Chief Ministers in several States.

In Rajasthan, where the Congress had lost majority, the Centre had proclaimed President's Rule. "The general elections in India show that when internal class struggle becomes acute, the reactionary rulers often throw to winds the sham 'democracy' which they use to deceive people." The "reactionary rule" was running into a serious crisis and "it is certain that revolutionary flames will rage throughout the vast territory of India." The review mentioned the two CPI (M)-dominated ministries, in Kerala and West Bengal, without much enthusiasm.[26]

[26] "After the Indian Elections: A Still More Reactionary Government," Peking Review, 24 March 1967.

Revolutionary Flames vs Parliamentarism

The CPI (M)'s assessment of the election results, however, was very much at variance with the CPC's. It did not, for instance, share the latter's optimism about the "revolutionary flames" raging throughout the country. The only basic point of agreement seems to be on the maturing political crisis. The CPI(M) saw in the defeat of the Congress a "qualitative change" in the situation "which should be characterized as the beginning of a political crisis."[27]   In objective terms it was a verdict against the policies of the government, that is the bourgeois-landlord classes bringing a new confidence to the people, facilitating acceleration and advance of the democratic forces in the country.

Its own key role in forming and running the non-Congresh governments in Kerala and West Bengal, the CPI(M) thought, was of "special political importance and significance" because the party could set the tone for other non-Congress ministries and force a new alignment and regrouping of democratic forces on higher political plane.[28] It was conscious of the limitations of the "class" state and the concentration of powers in the federal government and understood the two united front governments it was running only as "instruments of struggle." In class terms, participation in such governments was one specific form of struggle to win more support for the proletariat and its allies in the struggle for people's democracy, and at a later stage, for socialism.[29]

As it turned out later, the CPC did not regard the united

[27] Central Committee, CPI(M), *New Situation and Party's Tasks*, Calcutta, 1967, p. 39.
[28] *Ibid.*, p. 41.
[29] *Ibid.*, p. 70.

front government of Kerala and West Bengal even as "instruments of struggle" and attacked the very participation of the CPI(M) in them. Even the very first Chinese review of the post-election scene had made a lukewarm reference to these governments and had suggestively recalled that the communist-led ministry formed in Kerala in 1957 was prevented from carrying out even the few reformist measures it had proposed within the framework of the "bourgeois constitution" and was dismissed after 28 months.[30]

Now the CPC was in the CPI (M)'s participation in the system a gross revisionist tendency identified hitherto only with the pro-Moscow CPI. The CPI(M) was content to see sings of a maturing political crisis but the CPC saw "sparks of revolt glowing." A commentary branded the six-week old new Indian government a United States-Soviet Union pawn against China. "India's key position in the strategy of the United States imperialists and Soviet revisionists prompts them to spend freely and make all efforts to try and control India and enslave its people." The two big powers were trying to make India their military base against China. The commentary saw the one-party rule in New Delhi increasingly shaky, with the people forced more and more into violence to meet its tyranny, "angry masses" rising to seize food and arms in some States. The Naga and Mizo minorities were persevering in their anti-government armed struggle.[31]

Unlike the one-party communist ministry in Kerala (1957), the united front governments in Kerala and West Bengal were heterogenous, non-ideological quantities. These motely combinations included bourgeois and

---

[30] "After the Indian Elections: A Still More Reactionary Government," *Peking Review*, 24 March 1967.
[31] *Ibid.*

petit bourgeois parties, and groups and individuals. The only redeeming feature was the dominant position of the CPI(M) in these fronts. In Kerala the party held Chief Ministership but in West Bengal, though the largest constituent of the united front, it had surrendered leadership of the coalition to the Bangla Congress, a splinter of the Congress Party. There must have been considerable apprehension in Peking about the CPI(M)'s participation in these ministries especially in view of the party's ambivalent attitude to the peaceful transition issue. Yet it was too early to attack directly the CPI(M)'s participation in the united fronts with the attendant illusions of a peaceful transition to socialism through the parliamentary path.

Instead of attacking the CPI(M) directly, the CPC chose to put across its view in a roundabout way, making the pro-Moscow CPI the surrogate target. Chairman S. A. Dange provided the opportunity which the *People's Daily* seized. It attacked his 24 April statement to the effect that peaceful transition was possible in India and that the elections had changed the power structure, raising hopes of such transition. Dange had also said his party would seek talks with the CPI(M) and other parties for "an alternative government at the Centre" and to topple the existing once by peaceful means.

The fear that the CPI(M) might succumb to the temptations of the "revisionist" short-cut suggested by Dange seems to have prompted the bitter *People's Daily* denunciation afresh of the peaceful transition line. Dange's views were the "hackneyed phrases" of old revisionists Bernstein and Kautsky and modern revisionist Khrushchev and nothing but Indian version of "growing into socialism peacefully and winning a stable majority in Parliament, thus enabling it to realize the socialist transformation of society" theories.

The Soviet revisionist ruling clique has long dreamed of making India an "example" of "peaceful transition." Now, following the line of his Soviet revisionist masters and capitalizing on the fourth general election, the Dange clique has again dished up its "peaceful transition" garbage.[32]

The new Indian government was still "a reactionary regime of the dictatorship of the big landlords and big bourgeoisie." The non-Congress governments which had emerged in some States had not changed the "reactionary nature of the political regime." In the place of the Congress Party of the reactionary ruling class, the local feudal-comprador forces held sway from top to bottom in these non-Congress State governments.

On Kerala and West Bengal, where "Indian Communists hold part of the power," People's Daily said:

Nevertheless, these two State governments are component parts of the state apparatus of India's big landlords and big bourgeoisie. Under the direct control of the Central government, they are completely unable to either introduce any reforms in substance or shake the foundations of the capitalist and feudal relations of production. Furthermore, whenever the Central government deems it necessary, it can use the gimmick of "President's rule" to take over all State government functions.[33]

Thus the CPC's disapproval of the CPI(M)'s participation in the parliamentary system as a whole became un-

[32] "Dange's Plot to Sabotage Indian People's Revolution Will Surely Fail," Peoples Daily, 4 June 1967; Peking Review, 9 June 1967.
[33] Ibid.

mistakable. Short of calling for a people's war, the CPC suggested the alternative:

> These facts prove that without a people's revolution, without the seizure of political power by force and without the smashing of the old state apparatus there can be no change in the social system in the nature of the political regime, and there can be no real social reform. There is no precedent in history, nor will there be any in the future.[34]

The "Dange clique," taking advantage of the emergence of non-Congress governments in Kerala and West Bengal, was advertising the "Kerala path" and advocating a country-wide "united front" of the CPI(M) and itself. (In these two states, the CPI was sharing power with CPI (M) and other parties.) The "Dange clique" was also spreading the fallacy that peaceful transition could be realized easily and comfortably. "Their vicious aim is to make the Indian people give up their revolutionary struggle, lower their vigilance in the face of violent attacks from the Indian reactionaries and docilely accept their defeat."

The CPC's fight against revisionism was acquiring a new edge as the new Third World strategy was about to get off the ground:

> The Dange clique is the running dog fostered by imperial-ist and the Soviet revisionist ruling clique to sabotage the revolution in India.... To fight for their liberation, the Indian people must resolutely smash this renegade clique

[34] Ibid.
[35] Ibid.

and the revisionists of all forms and wage resolute revolutionary struggles.[35]

"Revisionists of all forms" outside the "Dange clique" obviously meant the section of the CPI(M) leadership which was sold on the peaceful transition idea and wanted to settle for parliamentarism.

Call for Armed Revolution

Within days Radio Peking openly called for an armed revolution in India.[36] This was to be followed by open support to the Naxalbari uprising led by members of the CPI(M) "who want to unfold a movement of 'deserting the united front government' and joining the Darjeeling struggle." These members, according to the radio, went to Naxalbari and other villages to lead and organize the peasants to carry out armed struggle for land "and thus took the road of China's revolution." The West Bengal government was the "tool of the Indian reactionaries to deceive the people and benumb their militancy."[36]

A broadcast two days later said the Indian Government was trying to put out the "revolutionary fire" in Darjeeling using the West Bengal government.

The tool of reactionaries, lauded by the renegade clique as a "non-Congress people's government," is loyally executing the counter-revolutionary orders of the Central Government, and has made a series of intensive preparations.[37]

[36] Radio Peking, 10 June 1967.
[37] Radio Peking, 27 June 1967.

The role of the West Bengal ministers in the "bloody suppression" and their attempt at a "political settlement" were
attacked. The climax of the campaign was the famous
article "Spring Thunder Over India."

The CPC was queering the pitch for the CPI(M) by
attacking the West Bengal government, thereby forcing it
to declare its position on Naxalbari. Either the united front
ministry, in which Politbureau member Jyoti Basu was the
Deputy Chief Minister, obliged the Indian Government by
crushing the movement or faced dismissal for its failure to
maintain law and order in the State. The CPI(M) could
no longer ignore the serious implications of the CPC's open
support to the "adventurists" of Darjeeling district who had
held a peasant conference in March 1967, declared that the
united front would not be able to solve the land problem,
and decided to launch a struggle that took the form of
clashes with the landlords and the State apparatus.

The CPI(M) now had to go beyond its earlier stand, viz.
that it was a struggle of the land-hungry peasants for land,
against eviction and for social justice and should be treated
as an economic problem. In the context of the open CPC
support to the uprising, M. Basavapunniah declared on behalf of the Politbureau on 2 July that Radio Peking's assessment of the Naxalbari struggle was at variance with his
party's.[39] In a signed article, Basavapunniah tried to establish that his party had no role in the uprising though the
"bourgeois-landlord classes and their hireling press" was trying to credit the CPI(M) with leadership of Naxalbari.
Basavapunniah denounced the "ultra-revolutionaries" who
openly assailed his party's programme and tactical line as

---

[38] Radio Peking, 29 July 1967.
[39] People's Democracy, 9 July 1967.

reformist and saw a well-laid conspiracy of the "big bourgeois-landlord government to isolate and destroy the
CPI(M)."[40]

Basavapunniah said the State government will treat Naxalbari as a peasant problem and not a law and order problem.[41]
The State unit of the CPI(M) demanded "halt" to massive
police action in Naxalbari, which it said violated the 5 July
decision of the Cabinet for the "restoration of normalcy"
by meeting the reasonable demands. The party was trying
to dissociate itself from the police action, so that it could
shift the responsibility for the repression and excesses on
other United Front parties. The Politbureau demanded
end to repression, stoppage of terrorization, release of all
peasants, stop to attacks on peasants, restoration to peasants
of lands in illegal possession, and stop to landlord violence
on peasants.[43]

The CPI(M)'s stance not only amounted to disowning
Naxalbari but abdicating its own political role in support of
the peasant demands. By acquiescing on police excesses
and repression the party was placing the survival of the ministry above everything. Its pronouncements amounted to a
candid confession that it was helpless vis-a-vis other united
front partners and a premium on staying in the ministry.
The plea that the police excesses were contrary to the 5 July
decision of the Cabinet lacked credibility because the Home
portfolio was held by Politbureau member Jyoti Basu.

The CPC's support to the Naxalbari uprising, without
directly attacking the CPI(M) but attacking the West

40 M. Basavapunniah, "Our Party's Stand on Naxalbari," People's
Democracy, 9 July 1967.
41 Ibid.
42 People's Democracy, 23 July 1967.
43 People's Democracy, 30 July 1967.

Bengal government aimed at pressuring the party into quitting the United Front. Finding the CPI(M)'s response to the situation disappointing the CPC moved a step further, extending the attack to cover "some revisionist leaders" of the West Bengal CPI(M) who were "opposing the revolutionary line of armed struggle" and persisted in following the revisionist line of peaceful transition.[44] More specifically, it was "those revisionist leaders of the Indian Communist Party who serve as Deputy Chief Minister or Ministers" in the State government for perpetuating the "fraud" or land reforms, and when it failed, agreeing to use of police force peasantry, and disowning the revolutionaries as "ultra left elements" and "adventurists."

The CPC seems to have calculated that majority of the CPI(M) following could be persuaded to revolt against the leadership and disown it. It turned fire on the actions of a "handful of revisionist leaders" in the party "in oppressing, deceiving and betraying the revolutionaries in the party and in sabotaging the revolution and oppressing the peasant movement." These revisionists were no better than those of "renegade Dange clique."

The question of armed struggle was posed again as the touchstone of the party's revolutionary bona fides. After setting up the area of armed struggle by Darjeeling peasants, "the real revolutionaries and real Marxist-Leninists in India will resolutely stand for armed struggle, lead and support it and thus gain the support of the broad masses of revolutionary people."

Naxalbari was not merely a struggle for seizure of land. It was a "struggle to seize political power," led by the

---

[44] NCNA report, "Indian Revolutionaries Say 'It's fine,' the Revisionists Say 'It's Terrible' to the Armed Struggle of Peasants in Darjeeling," Radio Peking, 1 August 1967.

peasant agrarian revolutionaries" of the CPI(M), guided by Mao's thought. The commentary harked back on Mao's famous observation in his Hunan report: "An awful mess!" and "Very good indeed": "The revolutionary people greet it [the Naxalbari struggle] joyfully with 'it's fine,' but some revisionists who retain their cloaks of 'communist' parrot the Indian reactionaries in crying 'it is terrible,' and stand in its way and fiercely oppose it."[45]

The CPI(M)'s weakness for the parliamentary system and its virtual repudiation of armed struggle irked the CPC, inviting sharper attacks. At the Army Day reception in Peking on 31 July, the acting Chief of the General Staff, Yang Ch'eng-wu, had referred warmly to Naxalbari. The NCNA followed it up with its own line: "The revisionists' betrayal and sabotage of the Naxalbari struggle had 'driven the revolutionaries to wage more resolute struggle against them'."[46]

Lessons of Telengana

Early in August, major Peking commentaries on the Indian situation were devoted to reviewing armed struggle in the past 20 years, underlining the lessons of the famous Telengana struggle and suggesting flexible guerilla tactics for the spreading peasant struggle. The Telengana peasant insurrection (1946-51) was perhaps the first application outside China of the Maoist strategy of people's war. The young communist leadership of the Telugu-speaking region in south-eastern India led the insurrection irrespective of the tactical line of the CPI in the rest of the country — right

[45] *Ibid.*
[46] NCNA, 2 August 1967.

reformism of the P. C. Joshi up to 1948 or the left-sectarian line of "intertwined revolution" of B. T. Ranadive between 1948-50, the Maoist line of C. Rajeswara Rao in 1950-51 or the amorphous tactics of the Ajoy Ghosh days until the struggle was called off under Soviet pressure in late 1951.

In all the post-Naxalbari reviews of armed struggle in India, the CPC has given the pride of place to the Telengana movement. 1953-55 anti-eviction struggles and the 1959-62 struggles for recovery of land lease and against high taxes, also mentioned in Chinese reviews, were of lesser order. The CPC saw in Naxalbari the resurrection of the Telengana movement. A review said that "the peasants of Telengana' and some other districts in south-eastern India once established a Red regime in an area embracing a population of nearly 10 million and carried out a large-scale armed struggle that lasted five long years...."[47] Under the influence of Soviet revisionism beginning with 1956, and because of the Indian revisionists' reluctance to work among the peasants, the movement was at a standstill between 1956-58. But spontaneous struggles broke out in 1959 and again during the famine years of 1964 and 1965.

All this show that as long as the feudal system of exploitation exists in the countryside, the fundamental contradiction between the landlords and peasants cannot be solved and the land problem has no solution. In such circumstances, resistance struggles and agrarian revolution are bound to take place and develop. After temporary setbacks new upsurges are sure to come. The armed struggle in Telengana had been betrayed and put down. But in a dozen or more years, the peasants in Darjeeling

[47] NCNA, 1 August 1967.

have risen and set up a Red area for carrying on armed struggle.[48]

An authoritative analysis of the Telengana struggle noted that for a long time, the Indian communist movement had witnessed an intense struggle between two lines. The revolutionaries had resolutely urged seizure of power through armed struggle, that is the path of the Chinese people who were guided in their victories by Mao's thought. "Some revisionist chieftains, however, have feverishly pushed ahead with the revisionist parliamentary road resulting in doing tremendous harm to the Indian revolution."[49] In 1946-51, base areas of armed struggle were established in Telengana where the landless and the land poor peasants were aroused to seize land by armed struggle "and become the banner of the Indian people's revolutionary struggle of the time." The analysis charged the "Indian revisionists" with betraying the Telengana struggle though Soviet intervention was mainly responsible for the switch and even the CPC was in a sense responsible for the abandonment of armed struggle.

The analysis went on to attack the "Indian revisionists" who had "manufactured fallacies that India is different from China, that time is not yet ripe for armed revolution in India, and that armed struggle is a form unsuitable for India. All this was done to cover up their revisionist parliamentary road and lead the Indian revolution astray." After a protracted struggle against revisionism, the revolutionaries "rekindled and held higher than ever before the torch of armed struggle" scoring an important victory against revisionism.

[48] *Ibid.*
[49] "Lessons of the Telengana Peasants Armed Struggle," NCNA, 2 August 1967.

The analysis claimed that the Telengana struggle grew
"under the radiance of the Mao-Tse-tung's Thought" though
the Indian revisionists vilified peasant armed struggles as
"adventurism and individual terrorism."

In a party document in September 1950 and again in an
open document in 1951, they vilified the Chinese people's
revolutionary war led by Chairman Mao Tse-tung, and
putting forward the theory of India's "exceptionalism,"
hysterically preventing the Indian people from taking the
road of the Chinese revolution.[50]

Long after the Telengana "sell out" and after many set-
backs the Indian peasants have realized the "futility of the
parliamentary path and the need for armed struggle,"

... the only road of victory of the Chinese revolution led
by ... Chairman Mao Tse-tung, the revolutionary road of
the proletarian vanguard going to the countryside and
leading the peasants in armed struggle, the road of building peasant areas in the countryside, encircling the cities
from the countryside and finally seizing power in the
whole country.[51]

The Darjeeling peasants had lit the "flames of armed
struggle" again.

A subsequent analysis, a more authoritative one, drew pointed lessons of the Telengana struggle. A *People's Daily*
commentator wrote that the "red torch" in Naxalbari illu-
minated the road of the Indian revolution to victory and

[50] *Ibid.*
[51] *Ibid.*

pointed to the direction in which it should advance. The history of the Indian revolution proved that where the "revolutionary line of Marxism-Leninism, Mao Tse-tung's Thought was dominant, a lusty revolutionary situation will emerge." Where a revisionist line gained the upper hand, the people will be betrayed and the revolutionary cause suffer a setback. Telengana was the triumph of the revolu-. tionary line. He saw a parallel between the "surrender" in Telengana and the tragic end of the 1925-27 revolution in China resulting from the "betrayal by opportunism and revisionism represented by Chen Tu-hsiu."[52]

Call for Maoist Party

The lesson for the CPI (M) following and revolutionaries outside it was clear beyond doubt: to build a Maoist party, by splitting the CPI (M) if need be

The revolutionaries in the Indian Communist Party and the revolutionary people of India should draw on the profound historical lessons of Telengana, drawing a distinct line of demarcation with the revisionist line politically, ideologically and organizationally and wage a resolute struggle against modern revisionism with the Soviet revisionist ruling clique at the centre. The revolutionaries in the Indian Communist Party will surely close their ranks in the struggle and build a *genuinely revolutionary* party of Marxism-Leninism, Mao Tse-tung's Thought.[53]

The CPC went beyond the call for a Maoist party for

[52] Observer, "Historical Lessons of Telengana Uprising," *People's Daily*, 3 August 1967; *Peking Review*, 11 August 1967.
[53] *Ibid* (italics added).

India. It underscored the primary condition for preserving the peasant revolutionary struggle—an army of the peasantry and rural base areas. The Naxalbari peasants had "won the first round in their struggle against ... encirclement and suppression" using native weapons (like the peasants of Hunan as observed by Mao Tse-tung in his investigation report). The Naxalbari peasants had proved that revolutionary forces had sufficient room for manoeuvre in the countryside and to develop and gain strength in the struggle. The Chinese revolutionaries had to go through the same test, "eventually building up a powerful people's army and large rural base areas and winning ultimate victory."[54]

The CPC was convinced that all the objective conditions for people's war existed in India and the subjective need was a Maoist party that would reject the peaceful transition line and get out of the parliamentary system. The victory claimed for the first round of the Naxalbari uprising was expected to take the peasant armed struggle to the next higher stage, of guerilla warfare and lead to the setting up of revolutionary bases all over the country. But the Naxalbari movement was crushed in no time. An account of the episode can be found in the "Report on the Peasant Movement in the Terai Region" by Kanu Sanyal,[55] a prominent leader of the Naxalbari movement.

Sanyal noted that peasants were the basis and the main force of the anti-imperialist and anti-feudal struggles in India. The peasantry of the *Terai* (the region on the Himalayan foothills in North Bengal where Naxalbari is situated) was part of the Indian peasantry. In the *Terai*, 70 per cent

---

[54] Commentator, "Let the Red Flag of Naxalbari Fly Still Higher," *People's Daily*, 7 August 1967; *Peking Review*, 13 August 1967.

[55] *Liberation*, November 1968.

of the peasants were poor and landless, 20 per cent were middle peasants, and 10 per cent rich peasants. The Naxalbari uprising stuck at the state apparatus of the comprador-bureaucrat bourgeoisie, and landlords and jotedars who represented feudalism, and established the rule of the peasant committees in the village throughout their armed revolt.

The revolt began with the call of the peasant convention of the Siliguri sub-division in March 1967 to (i) establish the authority of peasant committees in all matters of the village; (ii) get organized and be armed to crush the resistance of jotedars and rural reactionaries, and (iii) smash the jotedar monopoly of land ownership and redistribute the land through peasant committees.

The first step in the implementation of the plan was the creation of armed groups of peasants in the villages, in March-April 1967. The membership of the Kisan Sabha, barely 5,000 before the campaign, leaped to 40,000. Some 15,000 to 20,000 peasants were working full time to set up peasant committees through group meetings and to turn these committees into armed village defence groups. About 90 per cent of the villagers were organized. The committees carried out a ten-point programme in the villages. The first achievement was the destruction of the political, economic, and social structure of the village through an agrarian programme to redistribute all the land that was not owned and tilled by peasants. This, according to Sanyal, destroyed the feudal structure that had survived centuries.

The second, third, and fourth items in the programme were the destruction of all legal deeds and documents with the landlords, scrapping of all unequal agreements and mortgage deeds with landlords and moneylenders, and the confiscation of hoarded grain and work cattle and farm implements belonging to landlords.

The fifth was the public trial and execution of all the landlords known to be oppressors and opponents of the peasant struggle. Other achievements included punishment of the wicked, ruffian elements and flunkeys who propped feudal authority or co-operated with the police, arming of the peasants with traditional weapons like bows and arrows and spears as well as guns to resist armed repression through village defence squads; take over by peasants of the general administration of the village; constitution in every area regional and central revolutionary committees and replacement of feudal power by peasant political power.

The leadership of the struggle was with the landless peasants. The middle peasants' viewing the decisions of the conference with suspicion were not active in the first phase of the struggle. But when they realized that their enemy was the jotedars, landlords, and moneylenders, they joined the struggles. The rich peasants were critical of the conference decisions, opposed the struggle in the first phase and even spied for the jotedars. But when the middle peasants joined the struggle, the attitude of rich peasants changed. They gave up their opposition when the jotedars and the wicked people had been punished or driven out of the villages, and demanded justice from the peasant committees. The small jotedars split into two groups, one joining the struggle and the other turning inactive waiting for revenge.

Lessons of Naxalbari

Sanyal declared that the Terai peasant struggle was not for land but for state power, to overthrow by arming the peasants the comprador-bourgeoisie and the landlord class had come to terms with imperialism. The feudal landlord class was the main social base of the "imperialist and comprador-

bureaucrat bourgeois exploitation, and the peasants are the
main force and basis of this struggle." Herein lay the significance of Naxalbari, according to Sanyal. Without this
consciousness, any land struggle, however militant would be
mere militant economism.

The Terai movement according to Sanyal also solved the
problem of united front and its leadership in the anti-feudal
struggle. The tea garden workers not only participated in
the peasant struggle but were in its forefront, coming out
of the mire trade unionism and economism. From the anti-
feudal alliance grew up a genuine worker-peasant alliance.
This front cannot be led by any Marxist but only by a party
of the proletariat, with its own army and ability to build
a united front of workers, peasants, and petit bourgeoisie
and all those who can be united in the anti-imperialist and
anti-feudal struggle.

All the same the Naxalbari struggle could not advance
beyond a certain point. The reasons for this admitted set-
back, however temporary, were: lack of a strong party organization, failure to rely wholeheartedly on the masses and
to build a powerful mass base, old-line thinking, a formal
attitude to establishment of political power and revolutionary land reform. This was a struggle for state power and the
need, according to Sanyal, was to prepare the party and the
people militarily to the fullest extent, for as Mao had said
"Without a people's army the people have nothing."

Ignorance of military affairs and old ways of thinking
took its toll of the movement, which failed both politically
and militarily according to Sanyal. In the first stage, the
leadership underestimated the enemy's strength and later
overestimated it. It had a wrong understanding of Mao's
teaching in that it turned strategic defence into passive
defence.

Sanyal drew the following lessons from the *Terai* struggle: Mao's political and military theories needed deeper study; armed groups formed after arousing the villagers and arming them will become the village defence groups; knowledge of guerilla warfare should be acquired by arming the peasants with conventional weapons and organizing assaults on class enemies; liberated zones had to be built gradually by forming peasant guerilla groups. But without persevering in building liberated zones, formation of guerilla groups or their functioning would be difficult. The guerilla groups were to be the nucleus of the people's armed force.

The defeat of the struggle can be traced to two failure, in establishing revolutionary political power and in carrying out the land programme. The two achievements of the peasantry — the central zonal revolutionary peasant committees, and land distribution, were converted into most formal affairs thanks to the petit bourgeois weaknesses permeating the leadership.

Naxalbari was neither the first peasant armed struggle nor the first revolutionary base area in India and was no means the beginning of the Indian revolution. Even the CPC admits that the first armed struggle of the peasantry and the first Red area was Telengana in 1946-51. Unlike the Naxalbari uprising which was crushed, the Telengana movement was withdrawn under pressure from the Soviet-dominated Cominform and not defeated. Naxalbari is not the first peasant armed struggle after Telengana either, because the struggle in the tribal tract of Srikakulam district of Andhra Predesh had preceded the short-lived Naxalbari uprising but received national or international publicity. Unlike the Srikakulam struggle, the Naxalbari uprising took place in a State ruled by a United Front government with the participation of the CPI(M) and therefore acquired a special significance for the CPC. By its support to the Naxalbari uprising the CPC was symbolically challenging the peaceful transition line and underlining the compromise with opportunism implied in communist participation in the parliamentary system under a bourgeois constitution.

CHAPTER THREE

MAOIST PARTY
FROM ABOVE

THE IMMEDIATE OBJECTIVE of the Communist Party of China's call to the ranks of the Communist Party of India (Marxist) to demarcate themselves "politically, ideologically, and organizationally" with the revisionist line was not clear. If it was spliting the CPI(M) vertically or securing the overthrow of its leadership or forcing the party out of the parliamentary system and the peaceful transition line, none of these have been achieved even to this date. It was perhaps the CPC's hope that, ultimately, the Maoist stream of the Indian communist movement would prove stronger than the non-Maoist and all it wanted was to catalyze the process. The CPI(M) faced converging attacks on its programme and tactical line from the extremists within and the CPC without. The Naxalbari uprising had been put down but its spectre haunted the CPI(M) leadership. The challenge from incipient Maoism, though fragmented, was formidable.

The CPI (M) had come into being in 1964 not as a result of an ideological split or a Moscow-Peking polarization in the Communist Party of India which was already committed to pro-Soviet positions in the international ideological debate. What was witnessed in 1964 was more an act of secession than a split. The breakaway CPI(M) had left the ideological issue open and the mass detention of its functionaries and its preoccupation with the elections later had stood in the way of an ideological debate. But the party was now forced to join issue with the CPC on some immediate questions. Its Central Committee adopted two major resolutions in August 1967, one on the "left deviation" in the party and the other on its differences with the CPC, taking care not to suggest that the extremist challenge within owed its inspiration to the CPC's formulations on India. The first resolution rejected the "adventurists" and their line as "wrong, disruptive, and anti-Marxist" but admitted that many militant, honest, young members in the party were being drawn towards the "pseudo-revolutionary line" because it appeared to be militant. As a sop for the extremists, the resolution endorsed the 1952 tactical line of the united CPI which had made a formal commitment to armed struggle.[1]

The other resolution, "On the Divergent Views Between Our Party and the CPC on Certain Fundamental Issues" thought that the CPC had "practically come to the conclusion" that the CPI(M)'s programme was fundamentally wrong, that its assessment of the Indian political situation and the political-tactical line worked out accordingly were "reformist," that the CPI(M) was not a genuine communist party while the extremists expelled from it and all those rallying behind them were the real revolutionaries, and that CPI(M)'s political line was to be denounced publicly.[2]

The differences were of three categories: the class charac-

---

[1] "On Left Deviation or Left Opportunism," Central Committee Resolution adopted at Madurai, 18-27 August 1967, On Left Deviation, Communist Party of India, Calcutta, 1967.

[2] Central Committee Resolution, Communist Party of India (Marxist), Calcutta, 1967.

ter of the present Indian state and government, the actual
assessment of the economic-political situation in the country, and the principles governing relations between two
fraternal parties. The result of these differences was two
views on the stage and strategy of the Indian revolution.
The CPC's assessment led one to conclude that the new
Indian state was not "a bourgeois-landlord state led by the
big bourgeoisie which pursued the capitalist path of development with foreign monopoly capital" as seen by the
CPI (M) but "a puppet government led by bureaucratic
capitalism, run by them, principally in the interests of imperialism while reconciling themselves to live as parasites,
depending on the crumbs thrown by their foreign masters."[3]
On stage of the revolution depended the strategy and the
two assessments here were conflicting. A specific point of
difference here related to the appraisal of the Nehru government. The CPI(M) disagreed with the Chinese view that
the government represented the Indian bourgeoisie till 1959
but became the instrument of big monopoly thereafter and
abandoned its anti-imperialist role to became the lackey of
the anti-national big bourgeoisie, the big landlords, and
imperialism.

The CPI(M) also disagreed with the "highly exaggerated
and subjective" CPC assessment of the Indian situation. "It
is virtually negating our premise of a deepening economic
crisis and the initial stages of a political crisis, and in its place
substitution of the premise of an already mature revolutionary
situation and a revolutionary crisis, demanding the highest
revolutionary forms of struggle." Even if the objective conditions for revolution obtained in India, the subjective
conditions were absent. Particularly galling to the CPI(M)

[3] *Ibid.*

was the Chinese formulation attacking the non-Congress governments as the tool of India's ruling classes.

Undeterred by the CPI(M)'s resolution, the CPC went ahead with its denunciation of non-Congress governments and call for armed struggle. All parties and politicans in the nine non-Congress governments at the moment were "representatives of the interests of Indian landlords and bureaucratic-comprador capitalists," a commentary said. Under these governments, the relations of production were just the same as under the Congress party rule. Any attempt at a "democratic and peaceful solution" to India's land problem amounted to "Gandhi's doctrine of non-violence plus revisionist humbug."[4]

The CPC claimed an impressive record of gains for the first six months of its new Third World strategy. "The spark struck by Chairman Mao in the Chingkang mountains 30 year ago is spreading like a prairie fire through the vast lands of Asia, Africa and Latin America," a review of 1967 said. A "great storm of people's revolutionary armed struggle sweeping the world" was to follow sooner or later. The Asian people had realized the importance of establishing revolutionary bases in the countryside and such base areas had sprung up in Laos, Burma, Thailand and "other countries" becoming "strong bastions for the local people's revolutionary struggle." (Naxalbari was significantly not mentioned as a base area in the review.) The slavoes of China's Nanchang August First uprising (1927) were "re-echoing sharply" in the Third World.[5]

A lengthy article on India noted that the revolutionary situation was better than ever. The people were finally

4 NCNA, 13 September 1967.
5 *Peking Review*, 3 January 1968.

embarking on "the only correct road," the Maoist road of
seizing power by armed force. They were determined to
oppose armed counter-revolution with armed revolution.
"This is not only a great turning point in the history of the
Indian revolution, but is also of immense significance for the
development of the world proletarian revolution." The revolutionary line was winning one glorious victory after
another while the revisionist line of "peaceful transition"
(pursued by "usurpers" of the CPI(M) leadership, the
"renegade Dange clique and the handful of revisionist
chieftains whose representatives are Namboodiripad and
Jyoti Basu") has been steadily going on the rocks.[6]

Naxalbari-type peasant land struggles had developed in 50
places in eight states of India, the review claimed. The
"parliamentary road" had gone up in smoke and this was a
heavy blow not only to the Indian revisionists but to the
Soviet revisionist renegade clique and China's Khrushchev.[7]

A People's Daily article, credited to a "revolutionary mass
organization in a college," said Chairman Mao's road was
being followed in India and that was a "decisive factor in
the victory of the Indian revolution." The task was one of
arousing the peasant masses under the "leadership of a proletarian political party to carry out guerilla warfare and agrarian
revolution, to build rural base areas, encircle cities from the
countryside and finally seize them." The vast rural areas
were the "weakest link" in the reactionary rule. The peasant
struggles in the Darjeeling and other areas at present "have
prepared the ground-work for the establishment of a people's
army."[8]

[6] Peking Review, 12 January 1968.
[7] Ibid.
[8] "Mao Tse-tung's Thought Lights up the Way to Victory of
Indian Revolution," People's Daily, 16 January 1968.

The refrain was kept up. An authoritative analysis of the agrarian situation reporting Naxalbari-type action for land by force of arms in eight of the 17 Indian States went into lyrical ecstasy. "Growing in scale, the peasant struggle to seize land by force has assumed such proportions that, like thunderclaps and flashes of lighting breaking the dead silence of the overcast skies over India, it shaking the reactionary rule of the Congress government. An excellent situation, never seen before, has opened up for the Indian revolution. We warmly acclaim and cheer the revolutionary storm let loose by the Indian peasants."[9] After a graphic account of feudal exploitation and the growing resistance in the countryside, the commentator said the roots of the feudal system lay deep in the countryside. "Maharajahs, patriarchal landlords and the bureaucrat-comprador bourgeosie are the main social foundation of imperialist rule in India. This foundation must be overthrown if the Indian peasant had to achieve liberation. Indian revolutionaries have gone into the countryside to propagate Mao's thought that "political power grows out of the barrel of the gun."[10]

Ideological Debate

While the CPC's intermittent attacks on the CPI(M) programme and tactical line continued, there was no attempt at denouncing its long equivocation on the ideological issues facing the international communist movement. The ideological neutrality of the CPI(M) was untenable beyond a point and yet the CPC chose to ignore this and attacks were confined to its revisionism at home, and largely to a

[9] Commentator, "Let the Peasants' Revolutionary Storm in India Strike Harder," *Peking Review*, 1 March 1968.
[10] *Ibid.*

single issue, of peaceful transition. However, inside the CPI(M), the leadership was facing a serious challenge from sections of rank and file on the ideological issues, the debate on which was long overdue.

The Central Committee adopted a draft on ideological issues in August 1967 and released it for discussion. The draft was adopted at a special plenum in Burdwan in April 1968. But Peking chose to ignore this. The draft[11] was indeed a strange exercise. It examined the Soviet positions on all except one issue, and rejected them. The exception related to the issue of "unity in action" where the Chinese position was also examined and rejected. In sum, it was anti-revisionism sans Maoism because the draft generally took positions which lay somewhere between the Soviet general line and the Chinese general line. But for a solitary exception, the Chinese positions were not examined at all. Examined from Soviet positions, the draft can be termed anti-revisionist but viewed from Chinese positions, it might still be revisionist. The equivocation between Moscow and Peking (the draft called for simultaneous struggle against revisionism and left deviation) was to result in its isolation from the international communist movement for quite some time later. In the bargain, the CPI(M) lost the majority of its following in Andhra Pradesh. The draft was passed by paper-thin margins at some of the State plenums preceding the all-India pleum at Burdwan (by 12 votes in Kerala, by nine votes in Tamil Nadu) but in the Jammu and Kashmir plenum and the Andhra Pradesh plenum rejected it outright. The leadership's debacle in Andhra Pradesh was more serious because the State plenum had challenged not

[11] Central Committee Draft for Ideological Discussion, Communist Party of India (Marxist), Calcutta, 1967.

only the draft but as the Politbureau noted later, was declaring its fundamental opposition to "a whole series of basic questions concerning the Indian revolutionary movement as well as the international communist movement."[12] The plenum rejected the official draft (158 votes to 52, eight staying neutral) and demanded that a new draft be prepared by the Central Committee on the basis of the general line proposed by the CPC on 14 June 1963 and its nine comments on the CPSU's *Open Letter* of 14 July 1963, and also on the basis of the two resolutions placed before the plenum by T. Nagi Reddy and C. Pulla Reddy, and Kolla Venkiah, was based on an examination of all the issues related to the Indian revolution, on the basis of the CPC's general line and was a forthright attack on the "treacherous character of the Soviet revisionist leadership" which was weaking the international communist movement, the socialist camp, and the national liberation movements, and had become a "counter-revolutionary force."[13] It went into the class roots of Soviet revisionism.

The role of the national liberation movement in the new strategic environment was the central point of the Andhra documents and should have compelled Peking's attention. Of particular interest to the CPC should have been the reason for denunciation of the "unity in action" call on Vietnam, which was part of a deceitful Soviet move "to enter the ranks of Marxists-Leninists and in the ranks of the National Liberation struggles, so as to carry out greater dis-

---

[12] Politbureau, *Letter to Andhra Comrades*, Communist Party of India (Marxist), Calcutta, 1968, p. 1.

[13] *Andhra Plenum Rejects Neo-Revisionist Ideological Draft*, Vijayawada, 1968, p. 3. This collection contains texts of the Andhra Plenum's resolution, and the two resolutions by T. Nagi Reddy and C. Pulla Reddy, and Kolla Venkiah.

ruption."[14] A significant contribution of the Andhra documents to the ideological debate was their contention that
the contradiction with Soviet revisionism was an antagonistic
one and not only was unity between the Soviet and Chinese
parties impossible but at home, no united action between
the CPI(M) and the "Dange revisionism" was possible. The
party leadership was directly accused of compromising with
Soviet revisionism abroad and with "Dange revisionism" at
home. The Andhra plenum thus went beyond the ideological issues and reopened issues of the CPI(M)'s programme
and tactical line and attacked its participation in the united
front ministries, and in the parliamentary system in general.
The plenum tended to agree with the Chinese assessment
of the Indian situation, including the need for armed struggle.

The fight was carried on to the all-India plenum at Burdwan. According to a report, an Andhra leader ridiculed
the CPI(M)'s analysis of the post-1967 election situation
(the economic crisis maturing into the initial stages of a
political crisis)[15] as exactly the same as offered by General
Secretary Ajoy Ghosh at the CPI's Third Congress in 1953.
Instead of using the non-Congress governments in West
Bengal and Kerala as instruments of struggle, the party had
subordinated mass struggles to the preservation of these
united front governments. Mass struggles were breaking out
again in the country in spite of the formation of non-Congress governments and these were being met with repression.
The leadership, instead of resisting the repression, was curb-
ing the struggles in the name of preserving the legality of
the party. He also said:

[14] Ibid.
[15] Liberation, May 1968.

... we have not raised the perspective of the path of struggle from the point of academic discussion. Our movement in Srikakulam, Nalgonda, Warangal, Khammam are being subjected to intensified repression from landlord-goonda-police combine.... The question of resistance in this repression has come to the forefront. Because of a lack of clear perspective of the path of struggle, the leadership is not able to gear the party and the masses for resisting this repression, and take the movement to a higher level.[16]

The Andhra leadership's disillusionment stemmed largely from the curbs imposed by the party's current political line on the militant agrarian struggle the State unit was leading in the tribal tract of Srikakulam district and in some of the Telengana districts. Even when these struggles were growing into armed clashes, the all-India leadership was anxious to persist in parliamentarism and was afraid that these movements might cost the party its legality.

The Andhra revolt at Burdwan was quelled but, in the process, the party lost 60 per cent of its membership in the State. The extremists led by T. Nagi Reddy carried 11 of the 14 district Committees with them. In West Bengal, Kerala, and Tamil Nadu, the extremists were in a position to challenge the official leadership but were not in majority.

Revolt in Andhra Pradesh

The CPC's call for fight against revisionism and demarcation from it "politically, ideologically, and organizationally"

[16] Ibid. It was not until after the revolt at Burdwan that General Secretary P. Sundarayya wrote to the Prime Minister about the terror on the Srikakulam tribal people ("Savage Terror Against Tribals in Srikakulam," *People's Democracy*, 19 May 1968).

can be said to have found a substantial response, both in terms of quality and quantity, only in Andhra Pradesh. The State Committee had revolted against the all-India leader-ship. The Politbureau was to charge the Andhra extremists with staging the revolt under Chinese inspiration. Yet the CPC media did not so much as record the revolt of the Andhra Pradesh unit and its break with the CPI(M). This could only mean that the CPC, which in August 1967 had called upon the CPI(M) ranks to demarcate themselves from revisionism, was no longer keen on a vertical split in the party or forcing the isolation of its leadership but was content to limit its appeal to the revolutionaries outside the CPI(M).

Quite sometime before the Burdwan revolt, the extremists of West Bengal had set up a State-level co-ordination com-mittee of the revolutionaries of the CPI(M) and begun publication of a weekly Deshabarti. Similar co-ordination committees were formed in several other States by revolu-tionaries inside the CPI(M) to promote a line of struggle when it was found that the party's official line was turning more and more revisionist. In Andhra Pradesh, a State co-ordination committee was formed in September. In November 1968, on the initiative of the West Bengal committee, several State committees together formed an All-India Co-ordination Committee of Revolutionaries in the CPI(M). This was shortly after the CPC's call to Indian revolutionaries to "demarcate themselves from re-visionists."

The Andhra, Jammu and Kashmir, and several other State co-ordination committees had serious reservations about joining the all-India body and kept out of it. After its break with the CPI(M), the party's Andhra Pradesh unit began to function through State Co-ordination Committee.

Immediately after the Burdwan plenum, the all-India co-ordination committee which changed its name to "All-India Co-ordination Committee of Communist Revolutionaries" (AICCCR), reviewed the year since Naxalbari and renewed its call for building a true communist party through Naxalbari-type struggles "for revolution cannot be victorious without a revolutionary party."[17] It also called for boycott of elections and this negative slogan was to be followed by positive action, to mobilize and organize the people in "revolutionary class battles under the banner of Chairman Mao's thought" and to try to build a Naxalbari-type movement leading to a people's democratic revolution.[18]

Charu Mazumdar, the principal ideologue of the AICCCR, laid down the line in some detail. The contradiction between the peasantry and feudalism was the main one in the countryside and this can be resolved by peasant armed forces under the working class leadership setting up liberated peasant zones. This was the biggest and foremost task. All the parties had turned active accomplices of the enemies of revolution. The new democratic revolution can succeed only under the leadership of the working class and by following Mao's thought. A revolutionary party cannot be built merely by gathering various so-called Marxists who professed Mao's thought and had revolted against the leadership of their party, and declaring that a revolutionary party had been formed. The primary condition for building such a party was to organize armed struggle in the countryside. He said:

---

[17] "Declaration of the All-India Co-ordination Committee of Communist Revolutionaries," *Liberation*, June 1968.
[18] "Resolution on Elections," *Liberation*, June 1968.

...the old political cadres will no doubt be in such a party. But basically, such a party will be formed with the youth of the working class, the peasantry and the toiling middle class, who not only accept the thought of Chairman Mao but also apply the same in their own lives, spread and propagate it among the broad masses and build bases of armed struggle in the countryside. Such a party will not only be a revolutionary party but it will at the same time be the people's armed force and the people's State power. Each and every member of such a party must participate in struggles in the military, political, economic, and cultural spheres.[19]

Mazumdar, like the CPC, was placing a premium on new entrants to the ranks of revolution and minifying the role of those who had revolted against the CPI(M). Secondly, he was making the dangerous formulation that the revolutionary party will also be the people's armed force and the people's State power which implied all the three were co-extensive synonyms.

Thus there was intense confusion in the AICCCR about the priorities towards building a party and about the kind of party to be built. The frequent reiteration of the need to build a party through Naxalbari-type struggles was a vague and imprecise one. Several groups of revolutionaries in various States had left the CPI(M) or were about to leave it but had serious reservations about affiliation with the AICCCR. Agrarian struggles were breaking out in different parts of the country, notably in Srikakulam district of Andhra Pradesh where, beginning in 1959, it had grown into

---

[19] Charu Mazumdar, "The Indian People's Democratic Revolution," Liberation, June 1968.

mass action in November 1967, and into armed clashes later. In some of the Telengana districts of Andhra Pradesh communist revolutionaries had been leading similar peasant struggles. Movements on a smaller scale were on in Bihar, Uttar Pradesh, and Madhya Pradesh and the Calcutta-based AICCCR was claiming them though it was not leading all of them. In West Bengal, after the Naxalbari struggle (which had preceded the formation of the co-ordination), there was no peasant movement worth the name.

Problems of Party Building

Two important pieces of writing by Mazumdar measured his lack of clarity on approach to party building and the aims of Naxalbari-type struggles through which the party was supposed to be built. He had asserted that the Naxalbari struggle was not for land or crops but for seizure of political power.[20] But in practice, it lapsed into sheer economism, the cardinal sin of the revisionists. Mazumdar said the future of revolution depended on how quickly they built a party organization during the period and he expected an upsurge during the "coming struggle for seizure of crops."[21] While continuing to propagate Mao thought and policies, those who worked among the peasants should not belittle the need for common slogans — on economic demands. Seizure of crops was to be the "must" slogan to rouse hatred against the jotedars.[22] From armed struggle for political power, the peasant movement during the expected

[20] Charu Mazumdar, "One Year of Naxalbari," *Liberation*, June 1968.

[21] Charu Mazumdar, "Building a Revolutionary Party," *Liberation*, October 1968.

[22] Charu Mazumdar, "To My Comrades," *Liberation*, October 1968.

period of upsurge was to be whittled down to the level of seizure of crops and not even seizure of land.

The AICCCR meeting in October found that the ruling classes were using counter-revolutionary dual tactics (violent suppression of struggles and baits like mid-term elections and ministries). But the Naxalbari peasant struggle had already entered its second stage, "the stage of guerilla warfare" in various parts of India — Bihar, Uttar Pradesh, Madhya Pradesh, Andhra Pradesh. The major task of the revolutionaries was to plunge into work among the peasant masses and set up revolutionary bases. Other tasks (developing class struggle among other sections) were undoubtedly important but should be contributory and subordinate to the major, basic task of setting up bases.[23] The resolution was silent on the question of building a party and on the role of mass organizations.

Once again Mazumdar appeared confused about the methodology. Expounding his "revolutionary tactics" for advancing the peasant movement, he identified the propagation of Chairman Mao's thought and intensification of peasant struggles as the foremost task. Secret propaganda through secret meetings should replace open propaganda, demonstrations and meetings, which were revisionist forms. Revolutionary intellectuals should begin working underground among the peasantry so that they are forced to depend on the peasant revolutionaries. But nothing should be imposed on the peasants. There should be ceaseless propaganda among the peasants as a result of which it would be possible to raise a political cadre. The secret organization of such cadres was to become the party of the future. But his ap-

---

[23] "On the Indian Situation and Our Immediate Task," *Liberation*, November 1968.

proaches lapsed into economism once again. He wanted movements for seizure of crops. Unless a broad movement was developed and the masses drawn into it, seizure of power would take longer. Guerilla warfare was a higher form of peasant struggle under political leadership. Hence only through the successful application of four weapons—class analysis, investigation, study and class struggle can areas of peasant's armed struggle be created.[24] Mazumdar had nothing to say about the role of mass organizations and the accent was on a secret party.

The CPC was to pick up the "class analysis" theme of Mazumdar almost immediately. A review at the end of January 1969 said the Indian revolutionaries had been working to integrate Mao's thought with the "concrete practice of the Indian revolution." Summing up their experience, the revolutionaries were underlining the importance of investigation in the rural areas and applying Mao's thought in making class analysis. The review cited two articles in the Bengali weekly Deshabrati which exposed "the extremely feudal exploitation" and refuted the claim of the "modern revisionists" that capitalism was dominant in the Indian countryside.[25] But here, the CPC's view on the objectives of the Naxalbari-type struggles was at variance with Mazumdar's. He had said that the Naxalbari struggle aimed at seizure of state power.[26] So had Kanu Sanyal.[27] But the CPC saw in the Naxalbari struggles and in the movements

[24] Charu Mazumdar, "Develop Peasants' Class Struggle Through Class Analysis, Investigation and Study," Liberation, November 1968.
[25] "Revolutionary Struggle of the Indian People Grows in Depth," Peking Review, 31 January 1969.
[26] Charu Mazumdar, "One Year of Naxalbari Struggle," Liberation, June 1968.
[27] Kanu Sanyal, "Report on the Peasant Movement in the Terai Region," Liberation, November 1969.

in Srikakulam, Uttar Pradesh and Bihar peasant "armed struggle against brutal repression" and "struggle to seize land."[28] Many genuine Indian Marxist-Leninist were going to the countryside to mobilize the peasants for armed struggle.

Meanwhile, serious differences were developing between the AICCCR and the Andhra Pradesh Co-ordination Committee on the conduct of the armed struggle in Srikakulam district for which the AICCCR was trying to appropriate the credit. As early as March 1968, that is, a few weeks before the Andhra revolt at the Burdwan plenum, Radio Peking reported the Srikakulam struggle in the most glowing terms: peasants in Andhra State, "who have a glorious struggle of revolutionary armed struggle," had recently "rekindled the sparks of armed struggle under the leadership of the revolutionary group of the Indian Communist Party." It quoted a newspaper report that revolutionary peasants in Srikakulam district in Andhra Pradesh and the adjoining areas in Orissa and Madhya Pradesh states had unfolded a Naxalbari-type struggle.

Led by the revolutionaries of the CPI(M), the tribals had carried out several violent actions. They were stepping up the manufacture of bows and arrows as weapons to cope with the armed suppression by Indian reactionaries. In Parvathipuram in Srikakulam the tribal people have maintained several armed attacks since 1st February....[29]

[28] "Revolutionary Struggle of the Indian People Grows in Depth," *Peking Review*, 31 January 1969.
[29] NCNA report, Radio Peking, 7 March 1968.

Movement in Srikakulam

The Girijan movement in the 800-square mile tribal agency tract in Srikakulam, however, predates Naxalbari and is independent of it. From 1959, the communist had been building a broad-based organization of the tribals, the Girijana Sangham, and under its leadership carrying on struggle against feudal exploitation which included the worst features of serfdom and bonded labour together with the steady alienation of tribal land to non-tribals. The Girijans were told that only when a "new democratic revolution" started they could have an "autonomous region" of their own. The political education given to the Girijan cadre, which was part of the party's Srikakulam district cadre, included lessons on the Telengana armed struggle and its experience. But there was a lapse here and there was no widespread propaganda about the need for armed struggle to capture State power.[30]

The Girijan movement reached a new stage early in the rainy season of 1967 when the party began implementing items of the 10-point agrarian programme for the area. On 31 October 1967, landlords and their hired hoodlums waylaid some delegates to a taluk Girijan conference and even opened fire killing two. After a short spell of frustration the Girijans once again were on the move and more items of the agrarian programme were implemented. It was common for the Girijans to carry axes, bows, and arrows, and country-made guns whenever they went to participate in demonstrations. The Girijan movement moved to a higher stage, with the Girijans occupying land of the landlords and seizing their crops. There was clash with the police on 4

---

[30] Revolutionary Communist Committee of Andhra Pradesh, "On Srikakulam Girijan Armed Struggle," Mimeographed, 1969.

March 1968, culminating in the exchange of fire. The police began setting up special armed camps and carrying out raids against the Girijans, and on 4 March there was an exchange of fire between the people of Pedakarja and the police. Two Girijans were killed causing great demoralization in the movement.

The party was not prepared organizationally for self-defence or resistance when the armed police stepped up raids. At the State CPI(M) committee's meeting in March (where the State Co-ordination Committee was formed), it was felt that the question of resistance to the raids should be decided in consultation with the district committee. By the time the State leadership could hold discussions with the district committee, armed raids had forced most of the leaders out of the tribal tract. Armed police and the hoodlums had robbed the people of their produce, supplies of salt and grain, clothes, and their work implements rendering them destitute. The main problem was one of meeting the immediate material needs of the people so that they could start life anew. On the advice of the State leadership, the district committee decided to arrange for supply of the immediate needs, to get the cadre to re-establish its contacts with the masses, to protect the arms still in their possessions, and to make arrangements for imparting guerilla training to the leading cadre so that when the masses were on the move again, a struggle could be launched. The training was to be completed by May so that when the rains began in June they could begin a fresh round of struggle seizing lands of the landlords with the armed squads resisting the police and the hoodlums. The land problem of the agrarian revolution was to be co-ordinated with a protracted guerilla struggle.

The district committee thought minimum military training was not necessary before guerilla struggles were begun

and such struggles could be launched even when there was
no movement among the masses. But it was decided that
military training was necessary and there should be a move
ment that would draw the masses into guerilla struggle.
Another important decision was to extend the movement to
other tribal tracts in the district and in the adjoining Orissa
State because the area of operation (Seethampet-Parvati-
puram tract), was too small and had a good road system,
leaving the squads little manoeuvrability.

The cadres moved into action once again but the district
committee did not arrange for guerilla training immediately
and seemed to have had some reservations about it. So the
State leadership had to intervene. The district committee
agreed to complete arrangements for training for those who
were to lead the guerilla struggles, to keep the local militants
(men and women) ready to handle bombs, bows and arrows,
spears, and country-made weapons, and to direct the Girijans
to use these weapons for self-defence and resistance against the
armed police and hoodlum raids, loot and violence. The
State leadership emphasized the need to wait for some movement among the masses on issues like land and crops before
guerilla struggle could be launched. The district committee
was to report to the State leadership when conditions for
launching guerilla struggles developed and a decision on
launching the struggle was to be taken after that. Along
with armed resistance, preparation for higher forms of regular guerilla struggle was to go on. One batch of activists
was given guerilla training but there was some unavoidable
delay in training the second batch. Some ammunition was
collected for local armed resistance but no arrangements
were made by the district committee for resistance.

The Andhra CPI(M) unit had in the meantime revolted
against the all-India leadership and gone out of the party

shortly after the Burdwan plenum (April 1967), and was functioning through a co-ordination committee. The Andhra Pradesh co-ordination did not join the AICCCR immediately but had declared that "every Marxist-Leninist should help unification of all revolutionaries through the AICCCR."[31] But some members of the district committee, instead of concentrating on preparations for armed resistance and guerilla training, were establishing links with the AICCCR and carrying on a vicious campaign against the State Co-ordination Committee—through which the Andhra State CPI(M) was now functioning—on the issue of armed struggle in Srikakulam. The AICCCR had a group loyal to it functioning from Guntur district under Venkataratnam, known as the "Solidarity Committee for Naxalbari Peasants Liberation Struggle." This organization was working against the State Co-ordination Committee, which had begun a dialogue with the AICCCR as a prelude to affiliation with it.

This was the situation when the district committee met in the third week of September. Some district leaders said that the State leadership was neo-revisionist and opposed to the path of armed struggle, and saw political motives in the delay in starting armed struggle and for not joining the AICCCR. The district committee unanimously decided on armed struggle. It said police raids had been resumed in the area and thanks to the enthusiasm created by the cadre which had re-established its links with the masses during the lull, the people as well as the cadre were ready for armed resistance to the raids. Any delay here would mean isolation and demoralization of the cadre. So the district committee should be permitted to start armed struggle immediately, using hand bombs, country guns and bows

[31] Resolution, 29 August 1968.

and arrows for their present. The State Committee should give technical assistance to the district unit without delay.

This resolution seemed to mix up two things armed resistance and armed guerilla struggle. It already had clearance for use of hand bombs and bows and arrows for resistance. Its own June resolution had made this clear. But instead of reviewing the implementation of the resolution, the district committee was passing another. The district leadership had been clearly told in June that if there was a movement among the masses, a regular guerilla struggle can be started but the latest resolution was silent on whether there was already a mass movement. Resistance with hand bombs, and bows and arrows would help regular armed struggle and where armed resistance had already been organized, it would not take much time to start regular guerilla struggle. The district leadership had agreed in June to the use of hand bombs and bows and arrows for continuous armed resistance. Use of fire arms was an important part of military training and had to await completion of the training.

The second resolution was on the question of joining the AICCCR. It recalled the December 1967 appeal of the "Naxalbari comrades" to the revolutionaries in the CPI(M) to repudiate the party leadership. In May 1968, the AICCCR had appealed to the revolutionaries still with the CPI(M) and those in separate groups to join the co-ordination because existence of separate groups harmed the revolutionary movement. As a result of these two calls, several State Co-ordination Committees had joined the AICCCR but not the Andhra committee, which was "regrettable." The district committee decided to join the AICCCR and hoped the State committee would follow suit. An amendment to delete the sentence which said the

district committee agreed to join the AICCCR (because it
implied that the district unit was for dealing with the
AICCCR directly without functioning as part of the State
Co-ordination Committee) was defeated 4 to 3.

Factionalism and Armed Struggle

The Andhra co-ordination had basic ideological and organizational differences with the AICCCR and there were direct
talks on this between them. The Srikakulam district committee had been briefed on these discussions. But the
district committee's decision was extraordinary for more than
one reason. It was not as if all the other groups in the
country had joined the AICCCR and the Andhra State Co-
ordination Committee was the only one keeping out. For
instance there were five groups in West Bengal outside the
AICCCR. In Kerala, the Kosalaramadas and K.P.R.
Gopalan groups were still outside it and in Tamil Nadu one
group had kept out. The Jammu and Kashmir unit had
not joined the AICCCR. Secondly, the resolution did not
mention anywhere that the State Co-ordination Committee
was opposing armed struggle and this was the reason the
district committee wanted to affiliate itself with the
AICCCR. But later the district leadership was to accuse
the State leadership of a lukewarm attitude to armed struggle
and even failure to start it. Thirdly, the district committee
which in June had the clearance for armed resistance was
now asking for permission to start armed struggle and at the
same time was joining the AICCCR. Fourthly, the district
committee was seeking technical assistance from the State
Committee for armed struggle and was yet charging the
State Committee with opposing armed struggle. The district
committee began acting independent of the State com-

mittee even after the latter had joined the AICCCR and
this defiance was being abetted and encouraged by the
AICCCR. The State committee had already agreed to start
armed struggle in Srikakulam and had completed the
arrangements for guerilla training to new batches of active
cadre from the district. Thus armed struggle was not the
issue between the State and district committees. When
the district committee met on 8 October, the State committee representatives explained their resolutions but the
district committee rejected them and refused to have the
guerilla training. Some of the district committee leaders
directly contacted activists of other districts and tried to
wean them away from the State committee.

It is not known if the Srikakulam district committee
secured affiliation to the AICCCR. Even the State co-
ordination committee was not sure of the district committee's position.[32]   However, the AICCCR's journal
Liberation of December 1968 published a report on the
Girijan struggle, credited to "Srikakulam comrades." In the
meantime, the State committee had joined the AICCCR
and its representatives attended the latter's October meeting
in Calcutta. The State committee's journal *Janasakthi* reported the AICCCR resolutions including the one calling
for revolutionary bases in the rural areas.[33]   It also published
Mazumdar's article on building revolutionary party.[34]

The report from "Srikakulam comrades" was in effect a
veiled attack on the State Co-ordination Committee which
had already joined the AICCCR. The report was published

[32] *Ibid.*
[33] "Grameena Pranthallo Viplavasthavaralu Nirminchandi," *Janasakthi,* 9 November 1968.
[34] Charu Mazumdar, "Viplava Party Niramananni Chepattandi,"
Ibid.

without the knowledge or the consent of the State committee which had reason to believe that the district committee
was dealing directly with the AICCCR. The report drew
the following lessons from the Girijan struggle: (i) though
the basic issues like land and feudal exploitation were taken
up from the very beginning, the politics of armed struggle
were not propagated systematically and the economic struggles were not linked with the seizure of political power
through armed struggle and the movement had not proceeded beyond its democratic content; (ii) the masses were never
made to realise the need for repulsing the hoodlum attacks
organized by the landlords and the masses were never allowed
to proceed against the enemies; (iii) out of a fear that active
resistance by masses would invite a Government offensive,
the State leadership directed the cadres not to resist the
police attacks; (iv) the leadership did not co-ordinate
organizationally the mass actions, especially after the Pedakarja clash in November 1967; and (v) though the cadre
had the opportunity of learning from the experience of the
Naxalbari struggle, it failed to learn the lessons. The movement in Srikakulam would have been different had the
cadre learnt the lessons of the Naxalbari struggle.

The report underlined the need to study Mao and to
integrate his teachings with the concrete situation and
observed that the State Co-ordination Committee which
had "very recently" joined the AICCCR now had "access to
the rich experience of revolutionaries throughout India."
The Girijan masses had realized now, more than ever before,
"the inevitability of smashing the present order and building
a new one in its place." They had also realized that to meet
the armed offensive of the exploiting classes armed struggle
was the only weapon left, the report said.[35]

[35] "Srikakulam Comrades Report," Liberation, December 1968.

The State committee representatives who attended the AICCCR meeting in October had found that there were no basic differences between themselves and the AICCCR on the following issues: allegience to Mao's thought; character of the Soviet leadership; and rejection of the parliamentary path and recognition of armed struggle as the immediate form of struggle. Srikakulam representatives, who were present at the meeting on the invitation of the AICCCR itself, were briefed by the AICCCR representatives on their discussions with the State leadership.

In November, the State committee pointed out to the district committee that it would help preparation for armed struggle and conduct of armed struggle if it functioned under the State committee in keeping with the principles of democratic centralism. But the district committee rejected this and said it could deal with the State committee only on the basis of co-ordination and implement only the decisions it liked and on others, take its own independent decisions. Again, in December, State committee leaders discussed with the district secretary the tactics and measures to be taken after armed struggle had begun. The district secretary was told that the co-ordination would not be worthwhile if the district committee tried to have direct links with other districts and recruited for Srikakulam people who had worked against the State committee. Yet the district committee continued functioning as a rival State centre with the direct encouragement from the AICCCR which was violating all norms of democratic centralism by dealing with a district committee directly bypassing the State committee. When armed struggle was about to be started in Srikakulam the AICCCR wanted to deprive the State committee of any credit for leading it and claim the credit for itself.

"Warfare Through Warfare"

When the armed struggle began in Srikakulam towards the
end of December 1668, the AICCCR claimed that the
Girijans were learning "warfare through warfare" and launched a vicious attack on the State committee. A report pur-
porting to be from Srikakulam said that for the first time
the Girijan tribals were able to put up effective and sustained
resistance against their exploiters because they were now
being led by Communist revolutionaries guided by Mao's
thought. The Communist revolutionaries had laid down the
immediate aims of the armed struggle: to take away by force
hoarded grain and other goods from the landlords; to refuse
to repay debts and loans; and to overthrow feudal landlords.
Those who opposed these tasks with arms would be opposed
with arms. And then the insinuation that the State committee was opposed to armed struggle:

> The struggle has forced everyone to take sides making it
> impossible for anyone to remain neutral. This is proving
> particularly embarrassing for the wretched lot of pseudo-
> revolutionaries—the notorious Dangeites and neo-revision-
> ists. The twilight of political indecisiveness in which
> these double dealers can trade their shady goods most
> comfortably has vanished, exposing their ugly features for
> all to see.[36]

A subsequent report said that the Srikakulam struggle has
extended from the hilly regions to the plains and peasants
were propagating the politics of armed struggle, raiding the

---

[36] "The Revolutionary Girijans are Learning Warfare through
Warfare," *Liberation*, February 1969.

houses of landlords, and resisting the armed police. The peasant masses of the tribal agency area, led by the Communist revolutionaries were setting up their own revolutionary organization, the Ryotanga Sangrama Samithi which was "in embryo the organ of the people's political power in villages."[37]

Party from Above

Meanwhile, the AICCCR, on 7 February 1969, had decided to disaffiliate the Andhra State Co-ordination Committee, and the next day decided to form a Maoist party. According to Liberation, the resolution on the formation of a party was unanimous which means it was passed without the participation of the Andhra committee's representatives. They had been expelled the previous day and the first resolution was not described as "unanimous."

The AICCCR's resolution noted "basic differences" between itself and the Andhra Committee. Therefore it had been decided to treat the Andhra unit "as friends and comrades" outside the AICCCR. Their relations would be "non-antagonistic." The differences mentioned related "first and foremost" to loyalty to the Communist Party of China. The specific instance mentioned was the failure of the Andhra co-ordination and its leader T. Nagi Reddy to revise their view on the armed raids in November 1968 on two police posts in Kerala by a group of revolutionaries led by Kunhikkal Narayanan. Nagi Reddy had denounced it as the act of agent provocateurs. But later, the Andhra co-ordination's journal Janasakthi had published the Radio Peking's statement and the AICCCR's statement hailing the raids.[38]

---

[37] "Srikakulam Marches On," Liberation, April 1969.
[38] "Kerala Thirugubatu," Janasakthi, 8 February 1969.

The second issue was the divergent attitudes to Srikaku-lam armed struggle. The AICCCR held that "instead of owning and gloryfying it, the Andhra Committee simply accords it almost lukewarm support." This again is not borne out by facts because the State Committee had always owned the struggle as can be seen from the writings in its journal.[39]

The third issue related to the call for boycott of elections. With AICCCR such a boycott was a basic question of revolutionary struggle for a whole period but the Andhra Committee "still persists in taking it as a matter of tactics." Nagi Reddy had failed to resign his seat in the State Assem-bly before 1968 as directed by the AICCCR.[40] (Nagi Reddy did resign in March 1969.)

The second resolution, on forming a party, found the revolutionary situation in the country excellent, amidst growing unity of revolutionary ranks. But the complex political and organizational tasks of a fast developing revolu-tionary struggle can no longer be met adequately by a co-ordination committee and the need therefore was for a revolutionary party. "Without a revolutionary party there can be no revolutionary discipline and within revolutionary discipline the struggles can not be raised to a higher level."[41]

The resolution laboured to rationalize its volte face from its earlier stand against a hasty approach to the formation of a party:

[39] See especially "Srikakulam Zilla Ryotanga Sayudha Poratam," *Janasakthi*, 8 February 1969. Even after the State committee's dis-affiliation from the AICCCR, *Janasakthi* published a *Liberation* article on Srikakulam, on 8 March 1969.
[40] *Liberation*, March 1969.
[41] *Ibid*.

Idealist deviation on the question of party building arise as a result of the refusal to recognize the struggle that must be waged within the Party. The idea that the Party should be formed only after all opportunist tendencies, alien class trends and undesirable elements have been purged through class struggles is nothing but subjective idealism. To conceive of a Party without contradictions, without the struggle between the opposites, that is to think of a pure and faultless party is indulging in mere idealist fantasy.[42]

Mazumdar explained the decision at length in an article[43] and he was refuting and repudiating his own stand barely five months ago.[44] It was no longer a question of building a party through struggles but forming a party first so that the struggles could be developed. Between the AICCCR's call in October 1968 for setting up revolutionary bases and stepping up struggles and the decision to form a party, the struggle in Srikakulam was the only major achievement it could claim. There were minor struggles in other parts of the country but there was no qualitative change in the situation to warrant the decision to form a party in a hurry. Among the various Maoist groups and formations in the country (all of them were not inside the AICCCR) there was broad agreement on the stage and strategy of the Indian revolution and the need for a Maoist party to undertake the task and the differences related to the tactical line.

The All-India Co-ordination Committee of the Revolu-

[42] Ibid.

[43] Charu Mazumdar, "Why Must We form a Party Now," Liberation, March 1969.

[44] Charu Mazumdar, "Building a Revolutionary Party," Liberation, October 1968; also Charu Mazumdar, "The Indian People's Democratic Revolution," Liberation, June 1968.

tionaries of the CPI(M) formed in November 1967 (it later became the AICCCR) did not take upon itself the task of forming a party and therefore as it said in May 1968, "studiously avoided the mechanical process of convening a conference of the revolutionary comrades and forming a revolutionary party therefrom." Instead, its accent was on organizing revolutionary struggles and the task of co-ordinating them to enable a real advance towards forming a revolutionary party without which no revolution can be completed. Those attending the first meeting of the co-ordination did not believe that a committee representing various groups waging ideological struggles would serve the purpose of a party. Nor did they believe that the problem of party-building could be solved by the creation of a centre consisting of the representatives of various groups because the differences of opinion were "not confined to a few groups alone. There are innumerable comrades who belong to no groups and yet have come forward to take part in revolutionary politics." That would have amounted to imposing something on the revolutionaries. The co-ordination had only "taken the initiative of leading the class struggles and uniting the comrades who take part in them. This initiative is an indispensable prerequisite for party-building." Anyone taking similar initiative had equal right in it.

The comrades of the Co-ordination Committee are fully aware that, if what has happened in Naxalbari is repeated in several other areas, the question of party-building will not remain confined to the whims and caprices of a few comrades. That is why, the Co-ordination Committee has laid utmost stress on organizing. This is the real nature of the Co-ordination Committee and this is how it views the question of party-building.[45]

But as it turned, the question of party-building became the matter of the "whims and caprices" of a few. After its volte face, the AICCCR went ahead to convert itself into "The Communist Party of India (Marxist-Leninist)" on 22 April 1969. Thus a Maoist party was formed but the majority of Indian Maoists were not in it and the Andhra co-ordination, which according to the Maharashtra State Co-ordination Committee was "leading armed struggles in much bigger area than the total area in which the AICCCR claims to be organizing armed struggles,"[46] was excluded from the party.

Several Maoist groups which chose not to join the new party looked to the Andhra Maoists as an alternative focus. The Andhra Pradesh Co-ordination Committee met in a plenary session early in April and adopted its *Immediate Programme* and decided to reconstitute itself as the "Revolutionary Communist Committee of Andhra Pradesh," and had decided to speed up the "revolutionary tasks" that had to precede the formation of a revolutionary party.[47]

Fragmented Beginning

The Maharashtra Co-ordination Committee was among the groups that did not consider the CPI(M-L) a genuine or representative Maoist party and wanted the Andhra revolutionaries to take the initiative for forming a countrywide

---

[45] "The Co-ordination Committee of the Revolutionaries of CPI(M) Its Nature and Object," *Liberation*, May 1968.
[46] Maharashtra State Committee of Communist Revolutionaries, "On Differences with the All-India Co-ordination Committee of Communist Revolutionaries," Resolution, 15 June 1969.
[47] *Janasakthi*, 19 April 1969.

Maoist party. The Maharashtra committee had decided not to implement the decision of AICCCR to convert it into the State Organizing Committee of the CPI(ML). Instead, it decided to seek a discussion with the Andhra Committee and other like-minded groups. Its resolution, after its representative had made the Andhra leadership, provides an interesting insight into the AICCCR's functioning and failures and its ultimate degeneration in "an opportunistic, bureaucratic and phrase-mongering body."

The Andhra unit's break with the CPI(M) had unleashed a similar process in practically every State unit of the party, according to the resolution. The period also witnessed a great upsurge among the people, in some cases leading to armed revolt, sometimes led by communist revolutionaries, and sometimes spontaneously. But the struggles could not spread with the speed which they began and anti-Marxist-Leninist mistakes began piling up. The AICCCR did not prove equal to the challenge and could not combat and correct the mistakes. Worse, its various resolutions and pronouncements on its behalf upheld anti-Marxist-Leninist positions. Many leading comrades in the AICCCR refrained from any criticism in their anxiety to preserve the unity of the revolutionary ranks. "This attitude itself was anti-Marxist-Leninist, for any compromise in principle and failure to boldly repudiate and attack incorrect positions is nothing but sheer opportunism."

The worse was yet to be. "Certain leading comrades of Bengal who had taken the initiative for forming the AICCCR and who were in majority in it, started behaving in the same fashion as the 'Marxists' and Dangeists behaved in the past." Their factional activity extended to bypassing certain State Committees and organizing their own factions. There was a systematic campaign to malign Nagi Reddy and others who had expressed genuine reservations about the AICCCR's positions. The climax of the drama was the expulsion of the Andhra revolutionaries from the AICCCR due to "basic differences" on one hand and to call them "comrades and friends" and treat the contradictions with them as "non-antagonistic," on the other. Basic differences and a non-antagonistic relationship are irreconcilable entities.

The decision to form a party was announced, according to the Maharashtra committee, to confuse the rank and file and force them to accept the AICCCR as the sole leader of the revolutionary movement. This is quite probable because had the Andhra committee continued in the AICCCR, the Bengal group could not have dominated it.[48] As the biggest and the best organized Maoist formation with a mature leadership, the Andhra unit would have emerged an important force in the AICCCR and the party to be formed.

The two decisions — to expel the Andhra unit and to form a party — were almost simultaneous (the gap was just one day), suggesting an anxiety to exclude it from the new party. Even before it took a decision to expel the Andhra unit, the AICCCR had, as alleged by the Maharashtra committee, been organizing its faction in Andhra Pradesh by dealing with the Srikakulam district committee directly, bypassing the State Committee. The AICCCR gave no convincing reason for its decision to convert itself into a party and its decision, far from uniting the various Maiost groups only contributed to a fragmentation of the Maoist movement.

[48] Maharashtra State Committee of Communist Revolutionaries, "On Differences with the All-India Co-ordination Committee of Communist Revolutionaries," Resolution, 15 June 1969.

CHAPTER FOUR

SRIKAKULAM—YENAN
THAT FAILED

INDIA'S FIRST MAOIST party — the Communist Party of India (Marxist-Leninist) as it chose to call itself — was formed on 22 April 1969, hundredth anniversary of Lenin's birth and formally launched at a May Day rally in Calcutta. The CPI(M-L) was meant to be a rural-based, secret and underground party of a new style committed to evolving a mass line.[1] But the very manner of its formation was contrary to its proclaimed objectives. It was odd for a rural-based party to have been formed in India's biggest metropolis, and for a secret and underground party pledged to armed struggle to have its launching at a public rally. It was meant to be a party that believed in a new style of work, and in evolving a mass line "on the basis of taking and giving to the masses and constantly to raise the level of its under-standing"[2] but it was formed from above, by the All-India Co-ordination Committee of Communist Revolutionaries which was dominated by leaders of one State, West Bengal. There was broad agreement among the various Indian

---

[1] "Resolution on Party Organization," Communist Party of India (Marxist-Leninist), April 1969, (Unpublished).
[2] *Ibid.*

Maoist groups and formations on the stage (people's democratic) and strategy (armed struggle by the peasantry) of
revolution but the differences related to the tactical line.
Instead of promoting a discussion towards an agreed tactical
line and building a party through revolutionary struggles,
the AICCCR, repudiating its own commitments on the
manner of building a revolutionary party, chose to denounce
other Maoist groups, that is the majority Maoists. The
"outsiders" belonged mainly to the Andhra Pradesh Co-
ordination Committee (which later became the Revolutionary Communist Committee of Andhra Pradesh), the Laxman
Singh group in Bihar which was opposed to the Satyanarain
Singh group, to the group in Ganjam-Koraput region of
Orissa which along with the AICCCR's group was leading
a movement there, some groups in Uttar Pradesh, Punjab,
and Jammu and Kashmir, and Kerala. The attendance at
the AICCCR meeting had dwindled practically to those
who had been associated with the Naxalbari movement.

The AICCCR leadership appropriated Mao Tse-tung for
itself merely by declaring itself a party and branding all the
other Maoist groups "counter-revolutionary":

Today there are many petty bourgeois groups which pay
lip-service to Chairman Mao's thought and even to Naxalbari. The Party holds that many of these groups represent
a counter-revolutionary current within the revolutionary
movement. They preach the "historical inevitability of
groupism at this stage," "building the party from below"
and other anti-Marxist-Leninist ideas. Thus they try to
leave the task of building the party to spontaneity and
deliberately to seek to prevent the formation of a revolutionary Communist Party at a time when comrades
leading armed struggles in different areas feel the acute

necessity for it.[3]

The CPI(M-L) claimed to be a contingent of the international communist movement led by the Communist Party of China. The CPC in turn conferred legitimacy on the CPI(M-L) on 2 July 1969 by recognizing it as India's only genuine communist party, by publishing excerpts of its political resolution[4] in *People's Daily*.

The party claimed that the last 18 months had witnessed the unification of Indian revolutionaries on all the essentials of a programme, placing the immediate formation of a party on the agenda. But the party was formed without a programme or a constitution. At its inception the party claimed to place ideology and politics above everything else but had to wait a whole year before it could adopt a programme. The political resolution was supposed to sum up the unanimity on the essentials of the programme which covered the general plan of the Indian revolution.

The political resolution identified the contradiction in contemporary India as "between feudalism and the masses of our peasantry." The stage of revolution was that of people's democratic revolution, "the main content of which is the agrarian revolution, the abolition of feudalism in the countryside." To destroy feudalism, which along with the comprador-bureaucrat capitalism was one of the two props of imperialism, the people would have to fight the U.S. and Soviet social imperialism too.

The class alliance was to be: the poor and landless peasants, who constituted the majority peasantry, and the middle peasants and the working class. The working class as the leader of the revolution was to unite the peasantry to ad-

[3] "The Revolutionary Working Class Party is Born," *Liberation*, May 1969.

[4] *Liberation*, May 1969.

vance towards seizure of power through armed struggle. A revolutionary front of all revolutionary classes was to be built on the basis of the worker-peasant alliance. People's war was the only means by which an apparently weak revolionary force can wage successful struggles against an apparently powerful enemy. The basic tactic of the peasant struggle would be guerilla warfare. The party's task was not merely mastering the tactics but rallying all the other revolutionary classes behind the basic programme of agrarian revolution.

As for the party itself, it was to be: (i) one of armed revolution, rejecting the parliamentary path and therefore cannot be built in isolation from armed struggle; (ii) rural-based, to rouse the peasantry to wage guerilla warfare, unfold agrarian revolution, build rural-base areas, use the countryside to encircle the cities, and finally to capture the cities; (iii) secret and underground, keeping its main cadre underground but while learning to utilize all possible legal opportunities would under no circumstance function openly; and (iv) of a new style, integrating theory with practice and forging close links with the masses and practising criticism and self-criticism.

Its organizational priorities were: ideological and political building over organization and structure; training of revolutionary cadre in revolutionary activities; building of revolutionary base areas in the countryside instead of working in the cities; preparing the working class for leadership of the revolution instead of carrying on economic and cultural activities in the cities; organizing leading teams of the party over mass enrolment of members, that is, quality of membership over quantity. The party was to develop a mass line through criticism and self-criticism but there was no reference in the resolution to mass organizations.

Problems of Tactics

The differences betwees the various West Bengal Maoist groups and the CPI(M-L) at this stage related to one main issue and three other related issues. The main issue concerned the principal contradiction. According to the CPI (M-L), it was between the peasantry and feudalism and carrying the democratic revolution to finish was the first task. Completion of the anti-feudal task amounted to capturing the countryside. Charu Mazumdar, chairman of the party, however, has gone on record that, by pointing out the principal contradiction, they were not isolating it from other fundamental contradictions. There were four main enemies to be defeated and eliminated but to achieve this, the principal contradiction had to be identified.[5] Other groups seemed to think that the CPI(M-L)'s emphasis on the principal contradiction amounted to regarding it as almost the only contradiction and some of them thought imperialism was the main enemy and feudalism and the comprador bourgeoisie survived only by the grace of imperialism. The countryside, being the weakest link in the chain, would be the main theatre of struggle but the peasant struggle should be linked up with the struggle in the cities by the working class and the petit bourgeois elements against the comprador bourgeoisie and imperialism.

As for the forms of struggle, there were three specific issues in the debate: (i) Was guerilla warfare the only form of struggle? (ii) Was there any need for mass organization? (iii) Should the party be a secret organization? Mazumdar answered these question in detail defending his party against

---

[5] Charu Mazumdar, "On Some Current Political and Organizational Problems," *Liberation*, July 1969.

attacks of other groups and made some controversial formulations: (i) a mass organization cannot organize the agrarian revolution, only an underground party organization can do it; (ii) since there were different classes within the peasantry (poor, landless, middle, and rich peasants) an organization of the entire peasantry would be dominated by the rich and middle peasants; (iii) attempts at forming such an organization would promote a tendency towards open movements through open mass organizations, inevitably turning them into another set of leaders of revisionist mass organization; (iv) the leadership of the poor and landless peasants over the peasant movement can be established only through underground party organizations among peasantry; and (v) guerilla warfare was the only tactic for carrying on peasant revolutionary struggle and the poor and landless peasants can establish their leadership of the movement only by their guerilla warfare.[6]

Mazumdar also said that the peasantry as a whole did not participate in guerilla warfare. An advanced, class-conscious section of peasant masses started guerilla war and it might in the initial stages appear a struggle of only a handful of people. He hastened to point out that this kind of warfare had nothing in common with the other kind of guerilla warfare advocated by the Guevara, which was waged by the petit bourgeois intelligentsia and not the peasant masses. Besides, there was another point of difference. Che Guevara's warfare relied on arms and weapons but what the CPI(M-L) advocated depended on the co-operation of the masses.

A latter-day CPI(M-L) refutation of the "Che Guevarism" charge elaborated the party's attitude to mass participation and mass organizations. A *Liberation* article,[7] credited

[6] *Ibid.*
[7] "Our Path: Guerilla Warfare," *Liberation*, November 1969.

to "A Peasant Organizer," paraphrased Mazumdar's formulations but in the process found itself at odds with a *Peking
Review* article[8] reprinted in the same issue of *Liberation*.

The article by "A Peasant Organizer" recalled peasant
associations Mao had spoken in his famous *Report on An
Investigation of the Peasant Movement in Hunan*, and
sought to establish that these were secret organizations of
peasants which later became "the sole organs of authority."
He insisted that Kanu Sanyal in his report on the *Terai*
struggle had referred to the same kind of organization. Such
associations were revolutionary organizations and components
of the State power because they grew out of revolutionary
struggle and were based on armed power. It also quoted
Mazumdar to say that only after guerilla units had cleared
an area of "class enemies" by annihilating some of them and
forcing others to free the countryside should the party form
peasant committees.

But this was contrary to what had happened in Hunan.
According to the *Peking Review* article, the peasant movement in Shaoshan area, as in other parts of Hunan province
developed swiftly and under the leadership of the party,
revolutionary mass organizations like peasant associations,
women's associations and children's corps, were raised, and
mammoth demonstrations and meetings were held, height-
ening the people's morale.

To meet the needs of the struggle, the poverty-stricken
peasants in 41 townships in the vicinity of Shaoshan
rapidly joined forces and began making their own weapons
—spears which increased from about a dozen at the beginning to several thousand. We launched vigorous and

[8] Shao Yung-hung: "Hail Rising Revolution Storm of the Indian
Peasants," *Liberation*, November 1969.

sustained offensives against the local tyrants, evil gentry and the feudal landlords and scored one great political and economic victory after another.[9]

In Hunan, the peasant associations (nowhere has it been suggested that they were secret organizations) did not follow but preceded the offensive against the class enemy in the countryside while in Srikakulam, the Ryotanga Sangrama Samiti was set up in the red base areas after a campaign of annihilation. This was contrary to the Hunan experience.

"Annihilation" Theory

What Mazumdar had expounded may not be Che Guevarism but it certainly was not Maoism in the classical sense either. Mao had repeatedly stressed the mobilization of the masses as an essential condition for guerilla warfare. In Mazumdar's algebra, guerilla action by a handful to annihilate the class enemy came first and the mass mobilization second. It was assumed that the shock attacks on the class enemy by guerilla squads would arouse masses into action. The origins of the CPI(M-L)'s disastrous tactical line that liquidated the powerful Srikakulam movement lay in this controversial formulation.

The "annihilation" theory dates back to February 1969, that is a few weeks before the decision of the AICCCR to convert itself into a party, and was inspired by an abortive "guerilla action" in a Srikakulam village. Some 10 guerillas attacked a landlord's house but could not annihilate him. Mazumdar, struck by the event, is supposed to have said: "This should be our only method to arouse the peasant

9 *Ibid.*

masses." Mazumdar's theory is supposed to combine the
essence of the lessons of Naxalbari struggle with an application of Lin Piao's wisdom applied to Indian conditions.[10]
The whole party was born on the basis of this generalization
which was to set the tone for the party's political and organizational resolutions.[11]

The political resolution of the CPI(M-L) had given a
central call for guerilla warfare in the countryside. This
marked the second phase in the politics of armed struggle
because the call was for a new type of armed struggle. Back
in October 1968, the AICCCR had noted that the Naxalbari movement in the country had moved to the next stage
of guerilla warfare, and had called for revolutionary bases
in the rural areas. But the only serious attempt at setting
up a rural base was in Srikakulam district of Andhra Pradesh,
where the movement had predated Naxalbari and in origin,
was independent of Naxalbari. By November 1968, the
struggle in Srikakulam had moved into its second phase. A
report by the district committee on 24 February 1969 (that
is some two weeks after the AICCCR had "disowned" the
Andhra Pradesh Co-ordination Committee of Communist
Revolutionaries, known as the Nagi Reddy group) claimed
that the Communist Party in the area was leading armed
struggle for the seizure of political power. This suggested
that a party organization had come into being in the area
even before the AICCCR decided in February 1969 to convert itself into a party. Guerilla squad actions, to go by the
report, were limited to resistance to police raids and attacks
on police but there was no reference to annihilation of land-

[10] "Srikakulam Guerilla Struggle Extends to the Plains: A
Lesson," *Liberation*, November 1969.
[11] *Ibid.*

lords [12] A subsequent report from Srikakulam (26 May 1969, that is, after the formation of the party) however, claimed extension of struggle to other Andhra Pradesh districts where "armed guerilla action against the feudal landlords, seizing their property, crops and guns" had begun But it was not "annihilation" by terrorist groups yet. The report narrated the trial by a "people's court" in Srikakulam district of a policeman caught by the revolutionaries, the punishment to death of a landlord by 200 people assisted by a guerilla squad. "Not satisfied with his death, the peasants painted slogans with his blood," and brothers of the landlord's wives and other relative participated in the action.[13]

About this time, the Communist Party of China saw the Indian people on the road to armed struggle, applying Marxism-Leninism-Mao Tse-tung's Thought to solve the problems of strategy and tactics of the revolution. A Peking report on the revolutionary struggle blazing across the vast country referred to the Srikakulam movement which had spread to other areas in Andhra Pradesh, and to adjoining Orissa State. In Bihar and Uttar Pradesh, the "revolutionary peasants have organized themselves" to beat off the landlord offensives while a peasant revolutionary armed force had appeared in the jungles of Lakhimpur in Uttar Pradesh. In Kerala State, "the revolutionary peasants have also waged armed struggle." In reality, however, except in Srikakulam and some other areas in Andhra Pradesh, there was no "armed struggle" worth the name at this stage. A feature of the report was its strong accent on the need for mass participation. Naxalbari, it said had "set forth the question

[12] "Report on Srikakulam," *Liberation*, May 1969.
[13] "Srikakulam Struggle Continues to Spread and Develop," *Liberation*, June 1969.

of the important significance of establishing revolutionary
political power." Another important question Naxalbari had
raised was "to have confidence in and rely on masses and to
fully arouse them." It said:

> In Naxalbari and other areas, the Indian communist revo-
> lutionaries organized some 90 per cent of the rural popu-
> lation into the Peasant Committees. They warmly praised
> the creative power of the Naxalbari peasant masses and
> their important role in the democratic revolution. They
> also stressed the necessity to protect the initiative of the
> masses. Many fighters taking part in the Naxalbari strug-
> gle have studied Chairman Mao's works, and have reached
> a better understanding of the mass line.[14]

"Red Power" In Srikakulam

When the CPC was underscoring the importance of organizing "90 per cent of the masses" the CPI(M-L) was
embarking on an infantile adventure in the countryside, re-
sorting to the killing of individual landlords. The attacks
on landlords were not mass actions with the help of guerilla
squads but by a handful activists, euphemistically described
as "guerilla squads." Even as the party was claiming that
"red power" had emerged in Srikakulam, its activity in other
areas was lapsing into mere terror. Reports of developing
"peasants' armed struggle" in Uttar Pradesh and Bihar
referred to the killing of landlords marked by the party as
enemies and there was practically no reference to any agrarian
programme. The success of the movement in these areas
was measured in terms of "enemies" killed and injured. For

---

[14] NCNA, 10 May 1969; *Peking Review*, 16 May 1969.

example: "...between June and July...three guerilla raids have been made in Muzaffarpur district, killing 4 enemies and injuring 15."[15]

In Srikakulam the movement still retained its mass character though annihilation of the landlords was part of the programme. The Government had declared the tribal areas of Parvatipuram, Pathapatnam, and Palakonda taluks "disturbed" and police camps were set up all over. The CPI(M-L) saw in this a campaign of "encirclement and suppression," but maintained that the struggle had reached a new stage "with regular ambushing of the police." "Red" political power had emerged there.

> While a phenomenal expansion of the red area of revolutionary armed struggle is taking place in Srikakulam and various other districts of Andhra, red political power has come to exist in some 300 villages of the Agency area despite the vicious attempt of the enemy to encircle and suppress it.[16]

Terror-stricken landlords had fled the "red" area and government machinery no longer functioned. The guerillas and members of the village defence squads were protecting the people from police and the Ryotanga Sangrama Samiti (Peasant Struggle Association), the revolutionary mass organization of the peasants, was the new organ of State power running the administration, settling disputes and carrying on investigation about lands of those who had fled or had been annihilated. The Samithi was soon to undertake redistribution of land among the poor landless peasants.

[15] "Reports from Uttar Pradesh and Bihar," *Liberation*, July 1969.
[16] "Red Area of Revolutionary Struggle Expands in Andhra Despite Campaign of Suppression," *Liberation*, July 1969.

People's courts were functioning in the areas.[17]

In contrast to the stealthy "squad actions" to kill landlords in other parts of the country, the "annihilation" campaigns in Srikakulam drew widespread mass participation, to
go by this report about 400 people including women in the
annihilation of a landlord in Akkulapalli in Tekkali taluk,
and 1,200 to 1,500 people besides some guerilla squads in
the killing of a landlord in the Pathapatnam plains, within
six furlongs of a police camp. Several instances of this kind
were cited in the report.[18]

By August 1969, the CPI(M-L), which had recorded the
emergence of "red power" in Srikakulam a month earlier,
saw the "flames of people's war burning brightly" in the red
area[19] but the pattern of warfare was not strictly Maoist—
"annihilation" of class enemies to force the enemy to flee the
countryside. The next month, a visitor to Srikakulam, (his
ignorance of Telugu language and the Andhra region was
ill-concealed) reported[20] that Srikakulam was going the way
predicted by Mazumdar who had hesitantly asked about five
months ago "Srikakulam—Will It be the Yenan of India?"[21]
"The red political power which has been established in this
hilly area of Srikakulam has turned the whole district, nay,
the whole Andhra red. With the consolidation of this
power and as a result of the series of fresh guerilla actions,
the level of consciousness continued to rise. After the
guerilla actions had started, the Party gave the call for building mass organizations, and this gave birth to the Ryotanga

[17] Ibid.
[18] Ibid.
[19] "Flames of People's War Burn Brightly in Srikakulam," Liberation, August 1969.
[20] "Srikakulam Going the Way Predicted By Charu Mazumdar,"
Liberation, September 1969.
[21] Liberation, March 1969.

Sangrama Samiti,"[22] the visitor wrote with gushing enthusiasm but would have hardly known that the outside leadership which was imposing its line on Srikakulam and making
guinea pigs of the local revolutionaries would be liquidating
the movement within six months. It suited the CPI(M-L),
dominated as it was by Bengali leaders, to claim credit for
the movement in Srikakulam as long as it was going ahead.
The Andhra Maoists outside the CPI(M-L) were the target
of attack because they had not approved of the methodology
of the Srikakulam struggle. They thought the struggle was
unrelated to the people's needs and was not based on mass
participation. Upto this point, there was no peasant movement worth the name in West Bengal, the State of Naxalbari and the CPI(M-L) leadership, knowing that it had
no real rural base in West Bengal, was obliged to claim the
only base in the country as its. But the Srikakulam leadership had begun blaming the outside leadership, that is the
Bengalis, for the setback the movement had begun suffering.
From annihilation of the class enemy by the peasantry with
the help of guerilla squads, the operations had degenerated
into the mere guerilla attacks on individual landlords without any relation to a mass movement. Nevertheless the
CPI(M-L) was asserting that a people's army was in the
process of formation in Srikakulam.[23]

Decline of Srikakulam

The Srikakulam struggle began showing signs of decline
before it was a year old in November 1969. As the police
forces began closing in on the "red" area, the people, and

[22] Ibid.
[23] "Flames of Guerilla Struggle Burn Brightly in Srikakulam,"
Liberation, October 1969.

not the guerilla squads annihilating the class enemy, were
the target of police attacks and the resistance of the people
was smashed step by step. In late November and early
December 1969, 13 leaders like Dr. Chaganti Bhaskara Rao,
Thamada Ganapathy, Nirmala Krishnamurthy, Subbarao
Panigrahi, and Ramesh Chandra Sahu were killed in encounters in what was claimed to be the "red" area. According to the Central Organizing Committee, they found themselves "suddenly surrounded by overwhelming superior
forces" and went down fighting. Six leaders, Subbarao Panigrahi, Nirmala Krishnamurthy, Saraswati Amma, Ankamma,
Ramesh Sahu and Uma Rao. fell into the hands of the
police. The party called for annihilation of "as many class
enemies as possible" to avenge the killing of these leaders[24]
and this directive in turn led to further disasters.

As the Srikakulam struggle was petering out, the CPI
(M-L) tried to open new fronts in West Bengal. Since
Naxalbari there had been feeble movements in Uttar Pradesh[25] and in Bihar[26] and Orissa. The party also claimed
to be leading armed struggles in Punjab, Tamil Nadu, and
even in Maharashtra and the CPC's mass media endorsed
these exaggerated claims. A *Peking Review* commentary
extended qualified support to the "annihilation" movement
when it stressed reliance on the masses while reporting an-
nihilations: "Relying on the masses, the peasant guerillas
in Bihar have been active in unleashing a struggle to wipe
out enemy agents and despots, and this had greatly height-
ened the revolutionary fighting will of the broad masses of

[24] *Liberation*, January 1970.
[25] "Armed Peasant Struggle in the Palia Area of Lakhimpur,"
Liberation, April 1969.
[26] Satyanarain Singh, "Mushahari and its Lessons," *Liberation*,
October 1969.

the peasantry." [27]

The two most important struggles of the period were in Bihar (Mushahari) and West Bengal (Debra-Gopivallabpur) and the lessons the party drew from them are relevant to its tactical line. The reason for discouraging mass participation in the guerilla raids (which was common in the earlier stages in Srikakulam) could be found in a self-critical assessment of the Mushahari struggle. Though the guerilla force depended on the active support of the people, they were "now planning to reduce the extent of mass participation in guerilla raids for reasons of security and safety, and also for reasons of efficiency in fighting and retreating."[28]

It was argued that when the police had intensified patrolling and there was an "encirclement and suppression" campaign, smaller guerilla units were more effective and efficient than larger units. But these reasons advanced for reducing mass participation in guerilla raids were hardly convincing because the experience and the successes reported from Srikakulam in the earlier stages had pointed to the contrary, that is, the need for mass participation.

The other lessons of Mushahari were: the art of conducting political propaganda and building up of revolutionary organization in conditions of "encirclement and suppression" had to be mastered. In the past, the tactic was to send the main guerilla force to the neighbouring area to escape encirclement but the areas of guerilla struggle cannot develop into a political base area unless revolutionary work was continued. Two political tasks (propaganda and annihilation of

[27] "Indian Peasant Armed Struggle Rages Like a Prairie Fire," *Peking Review*, No. 38, 1969; reprinted in *Liberation*, November 1969.

[28] Satyanarain Singh, "Mushahari and Its Lessons," *Liberation*, October 1969 (emphasis added).

class enemies) and three organizational tasks (building up
the party, guerilla units and Kisan Sangram Samithies)
were to continue even amidst the heaviest police concentration. While the main guerilla force escaped, the party
committees and the Kisan Sangram Samithies had to continue their political and organizational tasks, which means a
part of the force was to be mobile, and another part
localized.[29]

This lesson of Mushahari gave a new dimension to the
"annihilation" tactic if only in theory because it regarded
"annihilation" a continuing task even after the main guerilla
force had escaped to the neighbouring area to avoid "encirclement and suppression." The other lessons were: the party
must have absolute faith in the landless and poor peasantry,
and it should work tirelessly to rally the middle peasants
around the banner of agrarian revolution.

Debra-Gopivallabpur Movement

The movement in Debra-Gopivallabpur area (Midnapur
district of West Bengal) which began in October 1969 was
led largely by the student cadres from Calcutta city. The
"annihilation" tactic, already tried with varying degrees of
success and varied consequences in Mushahari and Srikakulam, was applied here on the basis of a new understanding
of its potential. After the Naxalbari uprising in 1967, the
movement in Debra-Gopivallabpur was the only significant
armed struggle in West Bengal and was part of plan to link
up the movements in the Gangetic plains (Bihar and West
Bengal) with that of the tribal movement in Orissa and
Andhra Pradesh.

[29] Ibid

The Debra-Gopivallabpur armed struggle[30] was qualitatively different from the Naxalbari struggle. According to an observer, "the Naxalbari movement was something of a mass upsurge in which the spontaneity and mass initiative far outweighed the planning and discipline required of a revolutionary movement."[31] But in Debra-Gopivallabpur, to go by the Bengal-Bihar-Orissa border regional committee of the CPI(M-L),[32] the revolutionaries began with a vague idea of a Naxalbari-type struggle and had hoped that guerilla squads would emerge out of armed clashes for the seizure of crops. (Mazumdar had called for seizure of crops in October 1968.) In practice, they found that they could not do anything more than propagate the politics of seizure of power through armed struggle. By their pure economism and public demonstrations they were exposing the organization and inviting repression. The movement was groping for a line until Mazumdar spelt out his tactic of annihilating the class enemy.

The Bengal-Bihar-Orissa regional committee guiding the struggle decided on 21 August 1969 on an annihilation campaign against class enemies.[33] According to the local party unit, two courses were open after this decision. One was to mobilize the armed people to raid the house of the landlord and annihilate him, the guerilla unit completing its job while the people tried to seize hoarded rice. Or, the

[30] See Report by the Debra Thana Organizing Committee, CPI(M-L), "Revolutionary Armed Peasant Struggle in Debra, West Bengal," Liberation, December 1969, for a detailed account of the movement.

[31] Abhijnan Sen, "The Naxalite Tactical Line," Frontier, 4 July 1970.

[32] Deshabrati, 23 April 1970, report quoted by Abhijnan Sen, loc. cit.

[33] Ibid.

guerilla unit was to make a thorough investigation and annihilate the landlord at the right moment. The report
admits that the local units could mobilize the people to
support the guerillas only on the slogan of seizing rice,
which by Mazumdar's earlier norms should smack of crude
economism. Besides those who participated in the raid
would spread the news of the raid among others. The police
would have to deal with the masses and not a handful of
guerillas. However, it was decided that only the first raid
should be along these lines and the subsequent raids should
be by squads without mass participation. The premium no
doubt was on the second method.[34]

The first action was on 1 October and the second action
shortly after and are supposed to have "heralded the beginning of Red terror." The landlords could not be killed in
either of these raids but this struck panic among them and
many of them fled the countryside. The subsequent actions
were claimed to be more successful but, in the process, about
a hundred peasants went to jail. The object of course was
"to create Red terror to fight reactions's terror."[35] The
special significance of the Debra-Gopivallabpur movement
was that, like Naxalbari, it took place in a State ruled by a
United Front government which included the "revisionist"
Communist Party of India (Marxist).

According to the regional committee, though the very
first action did not succeed, it unleashed peasant initiative
which would not have been possible through mere propaganda work. The attempt of the report was to vindicate
Mazumdar's line. "With every action mass initative and

[34] Report of the Debra Thana Organizing Committee, CPI(M-L),
"Revolutionary Armed Peasant Struggle in Debra, West Bengal,"
Liberation, December 1969.
[35] Ibid.

class hatred of the peasants started growing and so did rise level of their political consciousness."[36]

It was claimed that two months of the movement brought thousands of peasants into armed action resulting in the seizure of crops. Many landlords had fled the countryside. People's courts tried the oppressors and the landlords who stayed on accepted the terms of the peasants. Then came the police action, described by the report as a campaign of "encirclement and suppression," forcing the guerilla squads to disperse over a wide area and carry on annihilation alongside political propaganda. This was what Srikakulam had also witnessed. If dispersal of squads and continuation of the annihilation campaign in one region brought thousands of peasants into armed action as claimed, it should have yielded similar results in other areas where the squads dispersed and carried on annihilation and political propaganda. The fact is, like the Srikakulam struggle, the Debra-Gopivallabpur struggle failed because wrong politics was in command. The power vacuum through the blitzkrieg action by the guerilla squads was supposed to have brought the area was not to last long. Killing of landlords was not exactly destroying a system. The revolutionaries in Debra-Gopivallabpur did not attempt formal redistribution of land but underlined the control of peasant committees of village affairs, including appropriation of crops. Seizure of crops was considered an important issue[37] but seizure of lands by annihilating the enemy or forcing him to flee should have been an even more important issue. Seizure of crops, in any case, cannot be deemed part of any basic agrarian programme. The "red" power that was supposed to have

[36] *Deshabrati*, 23 April 1970; quoted by Abhijnan Sen, *loc. cit.*
[37] "Flames of Guerilla Struggle Spreads to New Areas," *Liberation*, December 1969.

emerged in Debra-Gopivallabpur was of a much lower order than in Srikakulam, where the Ryotanga Sangrama Samithi was claimed to have attended to the agrarian programme.

Warfare Through Warfare

The CPI(M-L) claimed extension of its armed struggle, that is annihilation of landlords, to Assam, Tripura, and the Jalpaiguri region of West Bengal.[38] A new upsurge was claimed in Naxalbari, with the "annihilation" of three land-lords. But, meanwhile, Mazumdar summed up the experi-ence of the revolutionary struggles for the benefit of his following. Naxalbari taught six lessons (peasants fought for political power, not land or crops; they carried on armed struggle against armed attacks of the state apparatus; they relied on weapons they could make and snatched fire arms with the help of these weapons; they relied on themselves; they developed the struggle only by fighting revisionism which in turn was possible only through Mao's thought and only when the peasant masses grasped them). Srikakulam which followed Naxalbari taught that peasants can carry on protracted war only through guerilla warfare. Yet four ques-tions raised by Naxalbari remained. Mazumdar answered them.

(i) *Where to start guerilla warfare?* The conception that it can be started only in mountains and jungles was wrong. They can be waged in plains too and the Indian peasants had proved this. People's war can be started wherever there were peasants because Mao had thought that it can be waged only by relying on peasants.

(ii) *Is it possible to wage guerilla warfare without mass*

---

38 *Ibid.*

movement and mass organization? Neither of them was indispensable for waging guerilla warfare. Open mass movement and mass organization were a hindrance to development and expansion of guerilla struggle.

(iii) *On whom to rely for guerilla warfare?* The poor and landless peasants, and no other class, can wage this struggle. Wherever the petit bourgeois intellectual tried to lead the struggle, guerilla warfare had failed to develop and it could not be linked up with class struggle.

(iv) *How to start guerilla warfare?* Only by liquidating the feudal classes in the countryside, through the annihilation of the class enemy.[39]

The CPC was quick to endorse the conclusions reached by the CPI(M-L) on armed struggle, which it was claimed not merely for land but for state power. To end the monopoly of land ownership and feudal exploitation, it was necessary to establish new political power through armed struggle. Where armed struggle had been developed, "revolutionary political power at the basic level" had been established.[40]

In subsequent Chinese writings, the accent was on mass participation and the agrarian revolution. An article titled "Dawn of the Victory of the Indian Revolution," credited to the workers' commentator group of the Lanchow oil refinery, referred approvingly to the CPI(M-L)'s work in the countryside and said that the party's cadres were propagating among the peasants the truth that political power grew out of the barrel of a gun and

[39] Charu Mazumdar, "March Forward By Summing Up The Experience Of The Peasant Revolutionary Struggle Of India," *Liberation,* December 1969.

[40] "India's Revolutionary Armed Struggle Surges Forward," *Peking Review,* No. 44, 1969; *Liberation,* December 1969.

organized masses, armed them, mobilized them and brought their force into play. They conducted guerilla warfare with the close co-operation of the masses and in accordance with the concrete conditions in India. They attacked the landlords, overthrew their political power, repulsed the enemy's repeated "encirclement and suppression" campaigns, set up red revolutionary areas one after another and gradually built them into advanced revolutionary bases.[41]

The divergence here between the CPI (M-L)'s tactical line and the CPC's account of its implementation was unmistakable. The masses were not being organized and armed first to conduct guerilla warfare. Instead, guerilla squads were carrying out annihilation as a precondition for organizing the peasants. At least this was the rule outside Srikakulam where the peasants were already organized when the struggle reached the stage of guerilla action. The CPC accounts of Srikakulam conformed to the reality but its generalization about the CPI (M-L) organizing the masses and arming them first was not correct about other areas.

As 1969 ended, there was little doubt that the Maoist movement—of the CPI(M-L) as well as that of other groups—was growing extensively though the Srikakulam movement itself was heading towards a defeat. A *Peking Review* article claimed that the struggle was expanding, having spread already to 19 localities in 10 nearby districts. In 1969 there were 65 engagements between the guerilla squads and the police in Srikakulam. The CPC even credited Mazumdar with starting guerilla warfare in Srikakulam when the article said that he had "personally, kindled

---

[41] *Liberation*, February 1970.

the flames of the armed struggle in Srikakulam arriving there in March 1969 and instructing the district committee to build up guerilla squads and armed struggle immediately."[42] This should have lacked credibility for those who had heard a Radio Peking commentary a year ago, early in March 1968, about the Andhra peasants having "rekindled the sparks of armed struggle" and about the Naxalbari-type struggle unfolding in Srikakulam district in Andhra Pradesh and the adjoining areas of Orissa and Madhya Pradesh.[43]

Mazumdar wanted the 1970's made the decade of liberation, through the battle of annihilation which was to be sole form of struggle at this stage.

Select a particular area, a particular unit and a particular squad and then proceed to carry out successfully the battle of annihilation. Then select another unit and another squad, and carry on as before. In this way concentrate your work in one third of your selected areas and after our forces are consolidated in that part of the area spread the struggle to the remaining parts. This is the method pointed out by Chairman Mao, and this is the only correct method.[44]

Mazumdar also made available to the cadre a complete "murder manual" but surprisingly it suggested economic struggles (like seizure of crops) as a follow-up to armed guerilla action. Back in October 1968, he had pleaded for the combination of economic struggles with the politics of

[42] "Red Revolutionary Areas in India Shines Like a Beacon," Peking Review, No. 1, 1970; Liberation, February 1970.
[43] NCNA report, Radio Peking, 7 March 1968.
[44] Charu Mazumdar, "Make the 1970's the Decade of Liberation," Liberation, February 1970.

armed struggle. His new formulation therefore was extraordinary. The Debra-Gopivallabpur tactical line, and not
the Naxalbari or Srikakulam line, was to be carried out in
the future. The manual provided the inspiration for the
rash of murders that broke out in West Bengal in early
1970.

The manual in brief prescribed completely secrecy in the
formation of a guerilla unit and a wholly conspiratorial
approach to its action. The petit bourgeois intellectual
comrade should take the initiative here, approaching the
poor peasant who he thought had the most revolutionary
potential, and whisper into his ears: "Don't you think it
is a good thing to finish off such-and-such a landlord?" This
was how guerillas were to be chosen and organized into
units of seven, with utmost secrecy about their names, the
name of the landlord to be liquidated, and the time and
place of the action. In choosing the victim, they should
be guided by the will of the majority of the people. Guerillas
should make their own arrangements for shelter. No fire
arms were to be used at this stage. The guerilla unit had
to rely wholly on choppers, spears, javelins and sickles. The
reliance was to be on people and not weapons. The petit
bourgeois intellectual should sit together with the guerilla
unit to plan the attack in detail. The first attack was of
utmost importance and it was better to make several attempts than to make a hasty attempt and fail. Any rich
peasants cadre should be removed from the guerilla unit
before the first attack and if possible, the middle peasant and
petit bourgeois cadre too. A stage would come when the
battle cry would be "He who has not dipped his hand in
the blood of the class enemies can hardly be called a communist." The guerilla unit should disperse after the attack
The stage after the action was an important one because

political work had to begin here. Masses should be aroused on the basis of the action that had taken place. The guerillas should be re-mobilized on the basis of higher morale to carry out further annihilation. Such actions would lead to new guerilla units and the targets of attack would spread to new areas. The process would repeat itself and the mass participation would also increase. After the line of annihilation was firmly established, the political units should campaign for a broad economic slogan like seizure of crops.[45]

Thus the fight for seizure of political power was to be initiated by a few advanced elements and, theoretically, draw its strength from the initiative of the masses and mass actions, leading to people's war in the countryside. The CPI(M-L) invoked Mao in support of the "annihilation" line. The only reference Mao has made to annihilation was in the context of the anti-Japanese struggle, in December 1939, when he said "to emphasize armed struggle does not mean giving up other forms of struggle" and "to emphasize work in the rural base areas does not mean giving up our work in the cities and in the vast rural districts under the enemy's rule." Capture of the cities was the final objective.

This shows clearly that it is impossible for the revolution to triumph both the cities and the countryside unless the enemy's principal instrument for fighting the people — his armed forces — is destroyed. Thus besides *annihilating* the enemy troops in war, it is imoprtant to work for their disintegration.[46]

45Charu Mazumdar, "A Few Words About Guerilla Actions," Liberation, February 1970.
46 Mao Tse-tung "The Chinese Revolution and the Chinese Communist Party," Selected Works, Vol. III, People's Publishing House, Bombay, 1964, p. 86 (emphasis added).

Mao specifically meant the annihilation — and not killing — the enemy (that is, the Japanese occupation army)
and not any class enemy. About the feudal system, Mao
has said: "Our task is to abolish the feudal system, to wipe
out the landlords as a class, not as individuals."[47]

As for killings, Mao had a very cautious approach:

> After the people's courts have given the handful of archcri-
> minals who are really guilty of the most heinous crimes
> a serious trial and sentenced them and the sentences have
> been approved by the appropriate government organiza-
> tions ... it is necessary for the sake of revolutionary order
> to shoot them and announce their execution. That is
> one side of the matter. The other side is that we must
> insist on *killing less and must strictly* forbid killing with-
> out discrimination. To advocate killing more or killing
> without discrimination is entirely wrong; this would only
> cause our Party to forfeit sympathy, become alienated
> from the masses and fall into isolation. Trial and sen-
> tence by the people's courts, a form of struggle provided
> in the Outline Land Law, must be carried out in earnest;
> it is a powerful weapon of the peasant masses for striking
> at the worst elements among the landlords and rich pea-
> sants; it also avoids the mistake of beating and killing
> without discrimination.[48]

Mazumdar Against Mao

Mazumdar's annihilation line, patently un-Maoist came
under attack, not only from the various Maoist groups out-

[47] Mao Tse-tung, "One Some Important Problems of the Party's
Present Policy," *Selected Works*, Vol. IV, Foreign Languages Press,
Peking, 1961, p. 186.
[48] *Ibid.*, pp. 185-6 (emphasis added).

side the CPI(M-L) but within the party too. His leadership was being challenged by sections in the party. So he had to fight a two-front battle for his line. About the opposition from without, he wrote:

The emergence of social imperialism is but an episode in an era in which the world imperialism system is heading for total collapse. So, the various groups in India today, that have united to oppose the battle of annihilation by using the name of Chairman Mao, are also bound to fail in their attempt. This is the law of history. World revisionism is trying to unify these groups under the banner of spurious politics. This attempts of theirs is also bound to fail.[49]

The attack on detractors within the party had to be more subtle. An article credited to a faceless "Observer" began with a broadside on the "lackeys of revisionism" outside the party, that is the other Maoist groups and formations, hailed Mazumdar's annihilation line as a teaching of tremendous significance and the successful application of Lin Piao's guerilla war theory to Indian conditions and denounced those inside the party who were out to "prevent the battle of annihilation and thus obstruct the march of the agrarian revolution."[50]

The task, therefore, was "to establish firmly the authority of the leadership of Comrade Charu Mazumdar at all levels of the Party and revolution." The article admitted that despite party unanimity about guerilla struggle, there was

[49] Charu Mazumdar, "Make the 1970's the Decade of Liberation," *Liberation*, February 1970.
[50] Observer, "To Win Victory in the Revolution We Must Establish the Revolutionary Authority," *Liberation*, February 1970.

confusion and vacillation regarding the relationship between mass struggle and guerilla struggle and the respective import-ance of each. There was a tendency towards economism in spite of clear instructions by Mazumdar. Among the lapses cited were the inability to promote poor and landless pea-sants to leading positions in the party. If the party had to advance in the face of revisionist and reactionary attacks,

> we must conscientiously and seriously wage a struggle to establish the revolutionary authority of Comrade Charu Mazumdar. Our slogan is: Internationally, we must follow Chairman Mao, Vice-Chairman Lin Piao and the great glorious and correct Communist Party of China as well as the world-lessons of the Great Proletarian Cul-tural Revolution, nationally, we must be loyal to Chair-man Mao, Vice-Chairman Lin Piao, and the Communist Party of China and must fully accept the revolutionary authority of the leadership of Comrade Charu Mazum-dar.[51]

Thus the revolutionary authority of one person over the entire party, contrary to the norms of democratic centralism, was sought to be established. Party authority was being equated with the authority of an individual. A few weeks before the call to uphold Mazumdar's authority the leader-ship was fighting for demorcratic centralism and was attack-ing the elements which were recognizing the Central Organizing Committee but were defying the other commit-tees, which was a sign of revolt at the lower echelons:

> Under cover of revolutionary phrase-mongering quite a few people are raising the question: Well, the Central

---

[51] *Ibid.*

Organizing Committee is alright and we obey it, but as for the other committees, we don't recognise them. Though garbed in Left phrases this is a bourgeois individualist tendency, pure and simple, and as such a revisionist tendency.... Lack of faith in the authority of the Party breaks the backbone of the struggle.[52]

The CPI(M-L) nevertheless saw a qualitative change in its struggle, from the stage of primary guerilla activities to the stage of guerilla warfare against the armed forces of the government. In other words, a civil war situation was round the corner with the "Indian People's Liberation Army" on the point of being born to bring about a big change in the balance of forces.[53]

The differences over the annihilation line surfaced at the first congress of the party in May 1970, that is within a year of its formation. The organization report to the congress referred to the differences. Mazumdar, in his introductory speech presenting the report, elaborated the point and denounced "centrism" in the party as the "worst form of revisionism."

But by January 1970, the Srikakulam movement was all but finished and the police drive was succeeding. The local leadership had begun blaming the Calcutta-based central leadership for the set-backs and Mazumdar's pep-talks ("Srikakulam can never be crushed," "all the reactionary forces will be burned to ashes in the flames, kindled by the mas-

---

[52] Charu Mazumdar, "March Forward By Summing Up The Experience of the Peasant Revolutionary Struggle of India," Liberation, December 1969.

[53] Observer, "To Win Victory in the Revolution We Must Establish the Revolutionary Authority," Liberation, February 1970.

ses,")[54] notwithstanding, the struggle was fast losing its mass character. The guerilla squads dispersed over a wide area to escape the "encirclement and suppression" by the police forces and the people had to bear the brunt of the police repression, with no guerilla squads to protect them.

Within a year, the CPI(M-L) leadership managed to liquidate the decade-old Srikakulam Girijan movement, decimate the cadre and leave the people to the mercy of the armed police which conducted systematic raids on the villages. By mid-1970, India's Yenan-to-be of Mazumdar's dreams had been broken up.

[54] Charu Mazumdar, "The Peasant Revolutionary Struggle in Srikakulam is Invincible," interview to *Liberation*, March 1970.

CHAPTER FIVE

TWO SHADES OF
MAOISM

THE MAOIST MOVEMENT in India has had a fragmented beginning. The Communist Party of India (Marxist-Leninist) was formed from above by a group that was anxious to ensure its leadership of the movement and its claim to legitimacy rests on the circumstance that the Communist Party of China has conferred recognition on it and therefore it is the only genuine communist party in the country. But the CPI(M-L) is facing fragmentation now. Some of the groups which belonged to the party at the time of its formation have either gone out or been disowned. They are functioning independently, like the groups that had chosen to keep out of the party or had been excluded from it. The CPC's support to the CPI(M-L) and its tactical line has intrigued several Indian Maoist groups. In the absence of any other organized Maoist Party, the Chinese leadership might have found it expedient to support the CPI(M-L) to catalyze the revolutionary situation in India. The CPC has kept its options here because it has neither attacked the other Maoist groups nor supported them. However, a broad hint that it would be obliged to recognize other groups came late in 1969. A commentary on the Indian Maoist movement in the countryside said that "activists of the CPI(M-L) and other Indian revolutionaries have gone to work in places ... where class contradictions are acute."[1] The CPI(M-L)'s tactical line became counter-productive in the countryside even before it could hold its first congress in May 1970 and adopt a programme. Its activity shifted to Calcutta city and other urban areas following a call to counter white terror with "red terror," and this signified a major set-back to the party though the Maoist movement itself was striking roots in new areas.

In the long run the CPC might feel compelled to force a change in the CPI(M-L)'s style of functioning and its tactical line to put the party back on the rails. It might also attempt unification of the diverse Maoist formations in India into a single party on the basis of a common tactical line. In the past, the CPC has never spelt out the specifics of a tactical line for India. All that the Indian Maoists have got by way of guidance from the Chinese leadership was a general and vague but vigorous assertion of the Maoist revolutionary model. No doubt the CPC has supported the CPI(M-L) but not without subtle reservations and qualifications. The CPC's unfailing accent on mass actions — when the CPI(M-L)'s premium was on annihilation of the class enemy by a handful of revolutionaries — on the militancy of the urban people — when the CPI(M-L) believed in abandoning the cities as areas of "white terror" — etc., was perhaps meant as correctives to the wrong tactical line. Yet the CPC has not had a clear tactical line for India in view. It is possible that the CPC is baffled by the phenomenon of different shades of Maoism in India. The Andhra Pradesh Revolutionary Communist Committee (known as the Nagi Reddy group) provides an alternative focus to the Maoism expounded by the CPI(M-L) and its ideologue

---

[1] *Peking Review*, 31 October 1969.

Charu Mazumdar.

Before examining the two shades of Maoism, it would be well to recall the early Maoist phase in the Indian communist movement. The first recorded debate in the world communist movement on the legitimacy of Mao Tse-tung's teachings as part of Marxism-Leninism took place in India in 1948-49 and the first open denunciation of these theories as alien to Marxism-Leninism came from the General Secretary of the Communist Party of India, B. T. Ranadive. In the wake of the "left sectarian" deviation at the Calcutta (second) congress of the party early in 1948, the Andhra communists, who were already leading an armed peasant struggle in Telengana, turned to Mao's *New Democracy* in their search for an idiom for the Indian revolution and advocated the Maoist strategy based on a four-class alliance and a two-stage revolution with armed struggle of the peasantry as the means, for the Indian revolution. Ranadive who advocated the new-fangled theory of the "intertwining" of the democratic and socialist stages of revolutions wanted the entire Indian bourgeoisie to be fought. His polemic against the Andhra communists, who were the earliest Maoists in India long before Maoism came to be formalized as a strategy of revolution, had to extend to the very source of the Andhra heresy, Mao himself. Ranadive wrote:

> We must state emphatically that the Communist Party of India has accepted Marx, Engels, Lenin and Stalin as the authoritative sources of Marxism. It has not discovered new sources of Marxism beyond these. Nor for that matter is there any communist party which declares adherence to the so-called theory of new democracy alleged to be propounded by Mao and declares it to be a

new addition to Marxism.[2]

Ranadive was bracketing Mao Tse-tung with Tito and Earl Browder when he said it was "impossible for communists to talk lightly about new discoveries, enrichment, because such claims have proved to be a thin cloak for revisionism."[3]

The Indian communist movement witnessed a brief Maoist interlude when Ranadive was deposed as General Secretary and the young Andhra leadership gained control of the party. Cominform intervention in the form of an editorial in its journal[4] made the switch in the CPI's line possible and the new leadership withdrew the old leadership's unwarranted and "slanderous" criticism of Mao and the CPC. It also made a fresh assessment of the Indian situation after Liu Shao-chi had commended the Chinese model for other countries in the course of his address to the Peking conference of the Trade Unions of Asia, Australasia, and Oceania in November 1949. The manifesto adopted by the conference incorporated the CPC's line. The CPI leadership conducted a serious discussion on the basis of the Cominform editorial, the Peking manifesto and the works of Mao Tse-tung, among other things.[5]

Following the discussion, the leadership decided to "organize and facilitate the systematic study of the authoritative documents and the reports of the Chinese Communist Party, its history and the writings of its leaders" and to pub-

2 "Struggle For People's Democracy and Socialism—Some Questions of Strategy and Tactics," Communist, June-July 1949.

3 Ibid.

4 "Mighty Advance of the National Liberation Movement in Colonial and Dependent Countries," For a Lasting Peace, For a Peoples' Democracy, 27 January 1950.

5 "Statement of the Editorial Board," Communist, February-March 1950.

lish all these for the benefit of the party ranks. The leadership pledged "to the Communist Party of China, to its
leader Mao Tse-tung and to the international communist
movement" that it would "wage a tireless ideological struggle
against bourgeoisie nationalism and to steel the vanguard of
the Indian working class...."[6]

The early Maoist phase ended with Soviet intervention in
1951 when cold war replaced class struggle in its agenda and
the CPI was persuaded to abandon the armed struggle in
Telengana and to settle for peaceful constitutionalism.
Maoism has returned to India after nearly 20 years, in a
fragmented form.

The CPI(M-L)'s assessment of the Indian situation con-
forms to that of the CPC—that India is a semi-colonial and
semi-feudal country, with the obsolete semi-feudal base
acting as the social base of United States imperialism and
Soviet social imperialism, facilitating the plunder of the
people by comprador-bureaucrat capitalism. Of all the
major contradictions, the one between feudalism and the
broad masses of the people was the principal one in the present phase. The basic task of the Indian revolution was
the elimination of feudalism, bureaucrat capitalism, and imperialism. This determined the state of the revolution—the
democratic revolution, the essence of which was agrarian
revolution. The peasantry is to be the main force of the
people's democratic revolution, to be led by the working
class. The working class would rely on the landless and
poor peasants, firmly unite with the middle peasants and
even win a section of rich peasants while neutralizing the
rest. Only a small section of the rich peasants would join

---

[6] "Statement of the Editorial Board of 'Communist' on Anti-
Leninist Criticism of Comrade Mao Tse-tung," ibid.

the enemies of the revolution. Majority of the urban petit bourgeois and the revolutionary intellectuals would be reliable allies of the revolution while small and middle bourgeoisie, businessmen, and bourgeois intellectuals would be vacillating allies.

The democratic front for the revolution was possible only when worker-peasant unity was achieved in the process of armed struggle and after red power had been established at least in some parts of the country. The path of liberation was that of people's war and the working class can wage successful people's war by creating bases of armed struggle all over the country and consolidating the political power of the people through guerilla warfare which would remain the basic form of struggle throughout the period of the demorcatic revolution.[7]

The CPI(M-L) has set for itself three organizational tasks so that it can persist in armed struggle to achieve its programme ends: building and strengthening the party through criticism and self-criticism and links with the masses; a people's army under the leadership of the party; and a united front of all revolutionary classes and groups engaged in armed struggle under the leadership of the party.[8]

The Andhra Pradesh Revolutionary Communist Committee has no major difference with the CPI(M-L) over the general line or the stage of the revolution — a new democratic revolution to liquidate "the State of the big bourgeoisie, which is comprador and bureaucratic in nature, and feudalism." The programme can be achieved only through

[7] The analysis of the CPI(M-L) programme is based on the "Draft Programme" circulated among the ranks early in 1970 and adopted with a few minor changes at the party congress in April-May 1970.
[8] "Draft Constitution," circulated to the ranks early in 1970 and adopted with a few minor changes at the party congress.

a revolutionary line, the essence of which is the creation of guerilla bases in the rural areas which would encircle the cities. The united front to be formed against imperialism, feudalism and their collaborators, the big bourgeoisie, would be an action front in the revolutionary struggles and the armed liberation movement.[9]

The Andhra committee, unlike the CPI(M-L), does not regard the contradiction between feudalism and the masses as the principal one. Its accent is on the anti-imperialist task because it thinks that the main contradiction is between imperialism (including social imperialism) in alliance with feudalism, on one hand and the Indian masses on the other.[10] While the CPI(M-L) does not regard the national bourgeoisie a firm ally or a vacillating ally of the revolution, the Andhra committee wants the national bourgeoisie in the united front, along with the workers, peasants, and the middle classes. Further, while the CPI(M-L) is silent on the need to fight British imperialism and its references are limited to United States imperialism and Soviet social imperialism, the Andhra committee is more specific on this point and is therefore nearer the CPC's analysis which notes the importance of British imperialism in India.

The major differences between the CPI(M-L) and the Andhra committee relate to the tactical line, the methodology of revolution.

Matter of Methodology

As early as April 1969 the Andhra Pradesh Revolutionary Communist Committee (earlier known as the Andhra

---

[9] Andhra Pradesh Revolutionary Communist Committee, "Immediate Programme," unpublished document, April 1969.
[10] Andhra Pradesh Revolutionary Communist Committee, "Problems of People's War," reproduced in *Mainstream*, 2 May 1970.

Pradesh State Co-ordination Committee of Communist Revolutionaries) had expressed serious reservations about the methodology of struggle advocated by the AICCCR implemented by the Srikakulam district committee. Nevertheless it welcomed the beginning of armed struggle in Srikakulam:

> We have not received any authentic details about the armed raids carried on from the beginning of the armed struggle. Yet there is news that generally masses are participating in them. This is commendable. They, the district leadership which had broken off from the State committee may argue that it was the result of starting the armed struggle. But this is not correct. There was an indication of this development even in August and September 1968. Then we had not started armed struggle. These changes (of mass participation) are the result of waiting till the masses moved.[11]

Armed struggle had been started in Srikakulam on the basis of a strong peasant movement and its initial successes was not the result of the shock attacks on the class enemy by a handful of revolutionaries. A good beginning was not everything. The committee was justified in suspending its final judgment even as it extended all support to the struggle, and wanted it to advance along correct lines. It said:

> If the District leadership adopts correct tactic with correct perspectives and carries on the armed struggle, it would beat back the armed attacks of the ruling classes and

11 "Revolutionary Communist Committee of Andhra Pradesh, On Srikakulam Girijan Armed Struggle, April 1969 (mimeographed).

would be able to advance. We must carefully study the experiences of the Srikakulam struggle.[12]

When the committee reviewed armed struggle in the State three month later, the Srikakulam movement still had some mass character but was colliding fiercely with the State machinery. No thought seemed to have been given to the need for tactical retreats or consolidation of gains and the AICCCR's scattered following in other districts began implementing the Mazumdar line of shock attacks on the class enemy which was a euphemism for murder of land-lords by individuals and groups. Thus, alongside a mass movement in Srikakulam there were stray acts of terrorism in other districts. In contrast, the Revolutionary Commu-nist Committee had been conducting limited armed struggles where it had mass base in Warangal, Khammam, Karimnagar, Nalgonda, East Godavari and other districts while supporting the Srikakulam struggle. Its assessment of the Srikakulam struggle was:

... Without any other alternative methods to win their just demands, the masses of the Girijan areas have armed themselves and are advancing. to safeguard the movement they have built up and the gains they have achieved till now. Thus they are carrying on armed struggle and protecting their revolutionary movement and its gain. They are solving their land problems by cultivating their own lands. They are driving away the exploiters and liberating themselves from their exploitation. For the Girijan pea-sants, these are no small gains. When the armed forces of Government attempt to nullify these revolutionary

---

[12] *Ibid.*

gains and to suppress the organized movement, it has
become inevitable for the Girijans to safeguard them with
arms.[13]

The committee supported the struggles and pledged to
work for their complete success but it could not ignore the
dangerous trend that had set in under the CPI(M-L)'s
direction.

> ... some persons, forming themselves into groups and
> without any relation to mass movement, attack the land-
> lords and other exploiters. We want to make it clear
> that these attacks carried on without any relation to mass
> revolutionary movement cannot enable us to dissolve
> feudalism and carry forward the mass movement. Only
> through mass revolutionary rallies, revolutionary organi-
> zation and mass armed struggles we can dissolve the pre-
> sent big landlord, big bourgeois-imperialist system.
> Marxism-Leninism, Mao's Thought — all teach us this
> truth only. All revolutionaries should implicitly follow
> this. Viewed from this angle, it must be noted, such at-
> tacks by these groups are against Marxism-Leninism-Mao's
> thought.[14]

The CPI(M-L) which had gained leadership of the Srikakulam movement through the district committee was trying to establish the legitimacy of its "annihilation" line
as the precondition for organizing the peasantry on a mass
scale, by applying it, paradoxically, in an area which
already had a mass movement. This marked the beginning

---

[13] Andhra Pradesh Revolutionary Communist Committees, "On
Armed Struggle in Andhra Pradesh." Statement (mimeographed).
[14] Ibid.

of the third phase in politics of armed struggle in India. Even here, the tactic was bound to prove counter-productive beyond a point. This form of struggle the CPI(M-L) as the sole tactic even where there was no mass movement became the main issue of controversy later within the party. To begin with, it was the issue in controversy between the CPI(M-L) and the Andhra Pradesh Maoist formation (the Revolutionary Communist Committee). In a published interview its leader, Nagi Reddy, underlined the differences which involved not merely organizational issues but the whole philosophy of armed struggle. The first issue, according to Nagi Reddy, was the question of tactics in relation to people's war. Armed struggle started only as resistance to landlord goondas (hoodlums) and this was a form of people's resistance. Squads should be formed only out of this resistance. But the CPI(M-L) did not bother about this aspect of people's participation as a form of resistance to the landlord hoodlums and police repression. "Formation of squads even in areas where there is no people's movement at all is their methodology, which isolated the squads from the masses." Secondly, people's war always started as a form of resistance, not as a form of offensive. It was a battle in defence of their demands; it is through this form of resistance that a real people's army could be built.

But the methods of the CPI(M-L) has no relation to people's demands and people's struggle. Without any such relation, they go in for offensive action against any and every landlord even in places where there is no mass movement of any type. To put it simply, for us, it is a matter of resistance and for them, it is a matter of offensive.[15]

[15] Narayanamurthi, "The Srikakulam Story-II," *Frontier*, **20** September 1969.

The CPI(M-L) did not believe in any form of struggle other than armed struggle in any area, irrespective of its strength or mass following. This, in the view of the Andhra Maoists would not help build a mass movement even in areas where squad actions took place. Nagi Reddy's evaluation of armed actions in Srikakulam stressed mass participation:

Every action in Parvathipuram agency area and agencies of similar type is real people's action on the basis of a movement, which has been built up over number of issues including the basic question of land. People's participation is evident there and action against landlords is selective. But in the plain areas, generally there is neither a people's movement nor people's participation which can sustain those actions to develop a people's movement there in future.[16]

This naturally raised two other questions: was the Srikakulam armed struggle a national liberation struggle, and will actions of the Srikakulam type lead to armed struggle? Nagi Reddy said every armed struggle was not a national liberation struggle "immediately," though every struggle is an embryonic form of such struggle. To characterize every peasant struggle as struggle for power and national liberation was to divert attention and consciousness of the people from their basic demands. Only after a series of armed actions by peasantry in various places and their co-ordination into a people's army did national liberation struggle become a "fundamental form of struggle." Even Radio Peking had characterized the Naxalbari struggle as a struggle mainly for land and as an embryonic struggle for national liberation.

16 Ibid.

Srikakulam-type actions would not lead to armed struggle for two reasons. If people are not organized on their demands and made to win, mere squad actions would only divert their attention from the issues on which they had to fight. Secondly, people were their own liberators under the party's leadership, which meant they had to be part and parcel of the squads. But the CPI(M-L)'s methodology made the people feel that someone else and not they were the liberators.[17] The Andhra Maoist tactical line is based on an inseperable relationship between the party, armed struggle and the united front.[18]

Agrarian Programme

According to the Andhra Maoists, the beginning, development, consolidation, and the extension of all peasant struggles had to be based on an agrarian programme. Though complete liberation was possible only after the establishment of base areas, seizure of power throughout India, and the establishment of a new-democratic government, "liberation begins with the starting of anti-landlord struggle, with the starting of the agrarian revolutionary programme." In contrast, the CPI(M-L)'s line of "annihilation" implies postponement of the agrarian programme to a later stage and the destruction of the state machinery is the more immediate task:

Agrarian revolution is the *immediate task*. This task cannot be postponed and without it the peasants cannot be

[17] *Ibid.*

[18] The analysis that follows is based on three documents of the Andhra Pradesh Revolutionary Communist Committee, "Immediate Programme," *loc. cit.*, "On Srikakulam Girijan Armed Struggle," and "Problems of People's War," *loc. cit.*

benefited. But the agrarian revolution must await the smashing of state power. To attempt an agrarian revolution without first smashing the state machinery is straightforward revisionism.[19]

In keeping with this formulation, the CPI(M-L) did not undertake any agrarian programme in Debra-Gopivallabpur area in West Bengal where it carried out the "annihilation" campaign with some success. Agrarian revolution is not part of the people's war in the CPI (M-L)'s methodology. To the Andhra committee, agrarian revolution is the main content of people's war in principle and practice.

Peasant struggles to implement the agrarian programme would develop into armed struggle if the masses were trained and tempered to resist the enemy attacks that would follow such struggles. The programme of the agrarian revolution should be co-ordinated with intensive propaganda of people's war so that the masses understood the relationship between agrarian revolution and seizure of power. The masses should also be made to understand that the gains of their agrarian struggles could be protected only by wresting political power, which was possible only through people's war. "Thus by unleashing the abundant initiative and revolutionary potential of the vast masses a reliable mass base has to be built to start and carry forward armed struggle and develop it further."[20] The CPI (M-L) instead sought to create "base areas" by annihilating the class enemy: "When the guerilla units begin to act in this manner in any area the class enemies will be forced to flee from the countryside, and the

---

19. Charu Mazumdar, "Carry Forward the Peasant Struggle," *Liberation*, November 1969 (emphasis added).
20 "Problems of People's War," *loc. cit.*

villages will be liberated."[21]

According to the Andhra committee, this is at gross variance with Mao's concept of liberated areas. For, Mao had laid down three conditions for developing an area into a liberated or base area: building the armed forces; defeating the enemy; and mobilization of the broad masses of the people. As the Andhra committee understands Mao, building of armed forces means building of the people's armed forces capable of defeating the enemy's armed forces; defeating the enemy does not mean annihilation of class enemies but defeating the class enemy along with its armed forces; and mobilizing the masses means mobilizing and arming them against the class enemy and its armed forces in complete co-ordination with the people's armed forces.[22]

Two Lines

It was hardly surprising that there should have been serious differences in the CPI(M-L) over the annihilation line on the eve of its congress in April-May 1970. Charu Mazumdar's report to the congress refers to these differences and his speech presenting it admitted the existence of two lines of thinking in the party and any opposition to the official line was branded "centrist" deviation. The attack of centrism within the party, according to Mazumdar, came over questions of use of fire arms, dependence on petit bourgeoisie intellectuals and the annihilation programme. Mazumdar said annihilation was a higher form of class struggle and the beginning of guerilla warfare. Only through annihilation of class enemies would be born a new man who would rise

21 A Peasant Organizer, "Our Path: Guerilla Warfare," *Liberation*, November 1969, p. 74 (emphasis added).
22 "Problems of People's War," *loc. cit.*

above selfish interests, defy death, snatch away rifles from
the enemy and avenge the martyrs. Out of the process
would emerge a people's army. He ruled out the use of
fire-arms for the moment because that would dampen the
urge of the peasant masses to liquidate the class enemy
using conventional weapons or even "bare hands." But he
dreamt of the poor landless peasant marching with rifle in
hand at a later stage. He saw the possibility of a big mass
uprising in the country and the party's task was to create
as many points of armed struggle as possible, to spread
everywhere instead of limiting itself to any particular place,
and to extend the war of annihilation.[23]

As the party celebrated its first anniversary in April 1970,
its advance base in Srikakulam was crumbling, and the
squads had dispersed over a wide area to escape encirclement and suppression. A part of the hard core led by
Vempatapu Satyanarayana had shifted its base to the
adjoining tribal tracts in Orissa. In Debra-Gopivallabpur,
the movement was petering out as the police zeroed in.
The party switched its activities in West Bengal to the
urban areas, particularly Calcutta city, launching what
Mazumdar later described as "red terror" to counter white
terror. The campaign took the form of hit and run bomb
attacks on educational institutions, cultural centres, family
planning clinics, and government offices and desecration of
statues and portraits of national and religious leaders.

The timing of the terror campaign in the urban areas was
intriguing because a few weeks before the party's anniversary,
Mazumdar had advised the revolutionary students and youth

[23] The party congress documents and reports were published in
Deshabrati, Bengali journal published clandestinely. A report based
on these documents appeared in *The Times of India*, New Delhi,
19 July 1970.

to integrate themselves with the peasants and workers by going to the countryside in large numbers. Detailed instructions had been given to students to form small squads for work in the countryside even during short vacations, and particularly during the 12-week summer vacation about to begin. "Only when you have done this that you have passed your admission test as revolutionaries." He had also asked the students to form Red Guard units in different localities, schools and colleges and to swarm the countryside in thousands to work among the peasants and with the working class in the cities.

The Red Guards were to launch a major propaganda campaign, among other things, against "imperialist anti-China war plots" and to fight revisionism in general. The entire operational plan was Bengal-centred and was perhaps not meant for the rest of the country:

> The students and youth of Bengal have a glorious tradition. So, if you carry out this task of yours conscientiously I can assure you that the PLA [people's liberation army] will march in the sprawling plains of Bengal by the beginning of 1971, if not in 1970.[24]

The Red Guards were to meet fascist attacks in the cities and launch counterattacks.

If the nature of the red terror campaign was any indication, one part of Mazumdar's instructions (to the students and youth to fan into the countryside) was not taken seriously by his following while the second part of his instructions on work in the cities was carried out with dramatic results. In fact, the students already in the countryside

---

[24] Charu Mazumdar, "A Few Words to the Revolutionary Students and Youths," *Liberation*, March 1970.

could not withstand the police offensive and retreated to
the city of Calcutta mainly to elude arrest. The cadre in
the city tried to open a second front to ease police pressure
on the cadre in the countryside.[25]

The party's attitude to trade unions also underwent a
significant change on the eve of the congress. In the past,
all trade union activity had been held basically revisionist
and therefore futile. The party was against building trade
unions or capturing them. In any case, its premium was
not on mass organizations even among the peasantry because
that could at best lead to militant economism. The tactical
line of the past amounted to abandoning the cities as areas
of white terror and trade union work to the revisionists who
controlled the unions. The countryside was to be the main
theatre of struggle. Now Mazumdar laid down the new
line:

> We cannot oppose any struggle whatsoever waged by the
> workers against the class enemy. That would be petit
> bourgeois idealism. We will not make them dependent
> on us in any form of struggle waged by the workers for
> economic demands or against any attack by the employer:
> will encourage them with politics to take independent
> initiative.[26]

The party cadres would try to build secret party units
among the workers and some of the workers might be able
to provide leadership to trade unions and fight the revisionist

[25] An interesting account of this phase of the movement is found
in Sankar Ghosh, "Naxalite Tactics in West Bengal," The Times
of India, 19 May 1970.
[26] Deshabrati, 12 March 1970. Quotation as translated in Abhijnan
Sen, "Naxalite Tactics in Cities," Frontier, 3 October 1970.

leadership there but the prime task was to ensure that the workers did not develop revisionist tendencies.

The workers, who were to be encouraged in their struggles, were to be told nonetheless that weapons like the general strike and the hartal were no longer effective against the organized capitalist class and that struggles no longer develop peacefully or without bloodshed. "Today we will have to advance not in a peaceful, bloodless way but in paths such as gheraos, clashes with the police and the employer, barricades, liquidation of enemy agents—according to the situation."[27] Special attention was to be paid to agitations or other forms of struggle to support the workers if they were attacked.

The new style trade union work Mazumdar suggested provided another dimension to the red terror campaign. The revisionists, he said, had turned the gherao into Gandhian satyagraha. It was the duty of the party to turn the gherao into what it really was so that it can strike terror in the hearts of capitalists. Self-respect was to be inculcated into the workers so that they would outgrow the fear of losing jobs and even lives. If retrenched, they would become good party organizers in the city or join the peasant struggles in the countryside. Once a worker was inspired with revolutionary politics he would start militant struggles in the industrial areas to begin with and would even start killing the class enemies and their agents. But since Mao's thought would have taught him that the peasants fighting for seizure of political power were fighting his battle, the workers would go to the countryside to join the battle. The party organization was to launch and promote struggles on these lines.

[27] *Ibid.*

Red Terror Against White Terror

As it turned out, the main activity of the party, on this side
of the congress, was in the urban areas. The red terror
campaign by students was not a mere second front or a
passing phase to ease pressure on rural bases. The rural
bases collapsed and terror raids became the sole form of
party activity though sporadic killing of landlords in the
countryside continued. In the three months following the
congress in May, about 50 landlords were claimed to have
been annihilated in West Bengal and tally for the year was
150.[28] But the hit-and-run attacks in Calcutta on educational institutions and government offices, the burning of
the pictures and destruction of statues of Gandhi and other
"bourgeois" leaders, and the hoisting of red flag atop schools
and factories, got more publicity in the press than the
annihilation of landlords in the countryside.

According to a competent observer, there was no published theoretical justification of this movement though the
party's journal *Deshabrati* continued to support the student
actions and Mazumdar justified these actions later as on off-
shoot of the peasant struggle. The students were demolish-
ing the superstructure while the peasants were striking at
the base.[29] The party's Calcutta district committee decided
in July 1970 on a campaign of annihilation of the class
enemy in the urban areas, an extension of Mazumdar's line
for the countryside. Policemen, military personnel and big
capitalists and black-marketeers were to be annihilated to

[28] *Deshabrati* report, quoted in *The Times of India*, 21 Septem
ber 1970.
[29] Abhijnan Sen, "Naxalite Tactics in the Cities," *Frontier*,
3 October 1970.

avenge the death of the party leaders in Andhra Pradesh, West Bengal, and other States.[30]

In practice, however, annihilation of the class enemy in the urban areas meant attacks on individual policemen who were described as the agents of the class enemy. Until the end of September 1970, this was the main form of urban guerilla action and the party ruefully complained that the big business press was blacking out these achievements lest the police get demoralized.[31] The party was divided on the politics of killing policemen and Mazumdar who backed the action prevailed over others, notably Sushital Roy Chowdhury, chief editor of *Liberation*.[32]

The strategic objective of the killing of policemen was not clear though these acts were explained as support the peasant struggle in the countryside and fighting repression in the cities. Killing of policemen no doubt paralyzed the West Bengal police force by shattering its morale. This could be no means be construed as the creation of a vacuum in the cities or the destruction of the state machinery, just as the killing of landlords did not mean a vacuum or the destruction of the state machinery in the countryside.

In the meantime, the Srikakulam movement had been finally smashed in July 1970, when Vempatapu Satyanarayana and Adhibhatla Kailasam (who was to have replaced him shortly following differences between the all-India leadership and the district unit) were killed in an encounter. A few days later, two top leaders of Srikakulam, Chinna Appalausuri and Nagabhushan Patnaik, were held in Calcutta. The Srikakulam movement was now bereft of

[30] *The Times of India*, 4 August 1970.
[31] *Deshabrati* report quoted in *The Times of India*, 21 September 1970.
[32] Sankar Ghosh, "Naxalite Attacks on Policemen," *The Times of India*, 22 September 1970.

leadership, with the top men in jail facing trial or shot in encounters.

The severe set-back in Srikakulam compelled Mazumdar to think of a change in the tactical line and style of work. The functioning of the squads in Srikakulam was decentralized because, in any case, there was no central leadership left there. Each squads was to formulate its own plan and carry it out. The squads were to be small and scattered over a wide area and animated with the spirit of revenge. In Srikakulam, Mazumdar said, people had seized state power. Every village in the area was to have a revolutionary committee. The bulk of the members were to be from outside the party, from among the poor and the landless peasants. The party unit was not to interfere with working of the committee unless there were serious deviations. Mazumdar said that if this line was followed, Srikakulam would soon grow into a liberated zone from a mere red base that it had been in the past. The next stage in Srikakulam was to be the formation of the people's army which was to acquire fire arms (he had discouraged and even ruled out fire arms in the earlier stages of a movement), seizing them from the policemen who were to be annihilated by the guerilla squads. He visualized Vietnam-type struggle unfolding in Srikakulam within six months.

The decentralized squad functioning sanctioned for Srikakulam did not yield dramatic results and the movement lost its moorings in no time. The police had re-established complete control over the situation. The CPI(M-L)'s tactics had reached the dead-end in Srikakulam, which was to have been the "Yenan of India," and in another six months a Vietnam. Appalasuri and Patnaik had gone to Cal-

[33] Deshabrati article quoted in *The Times of India,* 4 August-1970.

cutta to discuss the serious differences between the Srikakulam unit and the all-India leadership over the conduct of the struggle and were arrested. Other Srikakulam leaders who had differences with the Mazumdar leadership were killed in encounters. The removal from the scene of Mazumdar's detractors and critics in the party was too much of a coincidence to be a coincidence and the mystery deepened with the arrest of Kanu Sanyal late in August because it was linked up with the reported differences between him and Mazumdar who had found West Bengal too difficult to operate from and had retreated to East Nepal. Radio Peking's commentaries on peasant armed struggle in India became less frequent, and in any case, less credible. After its set-back in Srikakulam, the CPI(M-L)'s shrank in stature to little more than a State party, its activity limited to West Bengal and its borders with other States.

The infantile phase of the Indian Maoist movement was drawing to a close towards the end of 1970, with no certainty that the CPI(M-L) would outgrow its Bengal-centered tactical line or that it would consolidate and preserve its gains in the countryside. The movement, led by petit bourgeois intellectuals, returned to Calcutta, abandoning the countryside and was degenerating into yet another petit bourgeois, urban phenomenon, trying to blend the Bengali terroist cult with Maoism as interpreted by Mazumdar. The party's base was practically limited to Calcutta city and its horizon did not extend beyond West Bengal.

In the rest of the country however, the Maoist movement has grown extensively though in a fragmented manner. Maoist peasant revolts in various isolated pockets of the country were spontaneous and independent of each other in the initial stages. The Srikakulam Girijan movement, for instance, predates the Naxalbari movement. The movement witnessed a phase of consolidation through the All-India Co-ordination Committee of the Revolutionaries of the CPI(M) because most of the leaders of these struggles were of the CPI(M), which later became the All-India Co-ordination Committee of Communist Revolutionaries. The phase of consolidation came to an end when a faction in the co-ordination tried to capture leadership of the movement by deciding to form a party from above. Nevertheless the Maoist peasant revolts in various pockets marked a turning point in the Indian communist movement. It was a decisive break with the parliamentary system to the lure of which both the Communist Party of India and the CPI(M) had succumbed and conscious attempt by the Maoist revolutionaries to reject the peaceful transition thesis and convert the struggle into a violent confrontation with the ruling classes by relying on the landless and poor peasants, farm labour and share-croppers. It marked the arrival of the politics of armed struggle, the politics of seizure of power through people's war.

Search for an Idiom

The Maoist movement which showed signs of consolidation until early 1969 had a faltering start, thanks to the infantile tactical line imposed on it by a section of its leadership. From advocacy of the formation of a revolutionary party through revolutionary struggles, this section of leadership effected a volte face and formed a party from above in contravention of all the canons of democratic centralism, just to make sure of its control of the fast growing movement. It wanted to appropriate for itself the credit for the Girijan movement in Srikakulam when it was reaching the stage of armed struggle. Having gained control of the Srikakulam movement, the leadership made the powerful tribal peasant base there the testing ground for its annihilation theory, with disastrous results. Annihilation of the class enemy in the countryside was central to the party's programme which included confiscation of the land and crops belonging to the class enemy, punishment of the agents of the class enemy, killing of the police, and organization of guerilla squads and people's liberation army for winning the people's war. But subsequently, the party bade 'goodbye to its agrarian programme announced earlier and struggles for seizure of land were condemned as a revisionist deviation. Annihilation of class enemies, which in the initial stages had mass participation, became conspiratorial squad actions and the war against the state machinery lapsed into clashes with governmental authority by a handful of revolutionaries. The CPI(M-L) began splintering with the set-backs it suffered when it implemented make-shift tactical line. The numerous splinter groups are groping for a tactical and functioning in isolation from each other. Nevertheless thousands of idealist youngmen are joining the ranks of the Maoist while more and more CPI(M) militants are turning to Maoism.

The chances of a strong, centralized Maoist movement re-emerging on a national scale depend largely on the luck of the CPI(M) with the parliamentary system. The pro-Moscow Communist Party of India has abandoned revolution and is content to function as a pressure group and a lobby for Soviet Union while the CPI(M), which still has the most militant cadre among the working class and the peasantry, has not rejected the parliamentary system yet despite its sad experience with the united front ministries in Kerala and West Bengal. The party found itself manoeuvred out of office in Kerala in October 1969 and isolated

and defeated at the polls in September 1970. In West
Bengal, the ministry dominated by it was dismissed late in
1968 but the 14-party alliance dominated by it returned to
office at the March 1969 elections, but broke up early in
1970. Its leadership has been under heavy pressure from
the militant following to quit the parliamentary system in
preference for extra-parliamentary methods of struggle. The
leadership has been quick to condemn the activities of the
Maoist groups as sheer left adventurism or to dismiss it as
anti-social activity thereby denying their political character.

In the absence of a credible Maoist rallying point,
thousands of CPI(M) militants are still in the party
functioning as pressure groups. The party is facing slow
crosion at both the ends. Those who believe in the parliamentary system and peaceful transition would profitably turn
to the CPI and those who believed in armed struggle would
naturally look to the Maoist groups. The consolidation of
the Maoist groups into a viable party would depend on two
developments—the accord among these groups on a tactical
line and a large-scale exodus of the Maoist elements from
the CPI(M).

Though the CPI(M-L) theoretically swears by the working class leadership of the united front for the new-democratic revolution, it has hitherto treated the working class
with contempt and has no working class base worth the
name even in West Bengal. In the name of its opposition
to revisionist economism, it had virtually boycotted trade
unions and kept out of working class action on economic
demands. The change in the line here early in 1970 has
not made much difference to the party's style of work among
the working class. The CPI(M), despite its weakness for
the parliamentary system can still claim the most militant
trade union cadre.

A viable Maoist party that might eclipse the CPI(M-L) in importance or might even emasculate it might yet emerge in the near future. The CPI (M-L) stake and fortunes are at best limited to West Bengal at present. It appears to be aiming at a red base in West Bengal by linking up its movement with the Maoist movement in the adjoining East Pakistan and with the ethnic revolts of the Nagas and Mizos in North-Eastern India which have the support of the Communist Party of China. But the Maoist movement in the rest of the country will not accept the petit bourgeois West Bengal leadership that dominates the truncated CPI(M-L). The inexorable experience of the Srikakulam debacle is there.

However unwittingly, the CPC, by its support to the infantilism of CPI(M-L), has contributed to the disruption of the Indian Maoist movement though it might have succeded in forcing large sections of the CPI(M) out of the parliamentary system. The CPC has to contend now with two shades of Maoism in India—one represented by the CPI(M-L) and the other by the Andhra Pradesh Revolutionary Communist Committee and the various formations agreeing with it. The CPC might well strive to achieve a single shade of Maoism in India by helping the movement make another idealistic beginning and to exploit the revolutionary potential which has existed for quite some time.

POSTSCRIPT

Since the completion of the foregoing chapter, the Communist Party of India (Marxist-Leninist) has been lashed by a new wave of dissidence over its tactical line. It is now a truncated, many splintered organization, with more and more State units asserting their autonomy in their tactics and rejecting the line of "annihilation" of the class enemy.

The annihilation campaign which fled the West Bengal countryside in May 1969 to the asphalt jungle of Calcutta, India's biggest metropolis, stays put there. The low-level urban guerilla warfare the city has witnessed is not complimentary to any guerilla movement in the countryside and has little to do with any mass movement or the goal of building a guerilla infrastructure in the countryside or to an agrarian programme. The annihilation line in being abandoned or its legitimacy challenged by more and more State units. Even Peking seems to have developed serious reservations about the line and more particularly, the CPI (M-L)'s application of the line Calcutta. A Radio Peking review of the "flames of revolutionary struggle in South-east Asia" made but a ritualistic reference to the CPI(M-L)'s movement in India but the accent was on agrarian revolution, which the party had abandoned. There was no reference to the "red" terror campaign in Calcutta.

In India, with a population of 500 million the revolutionary people under the leadership of the Communist Party of India (Marxist-Leninist) have for the past two years waged peasant armed struggle with agrarian revolution as its centre. This year cadres of the Communist Party of India (Marxist-Leninist) have gone deep into the vast rural areas where the struggle is most acute to further mobilize and organize the peasant masses and unfold guerilla warfare.

With the active support and co-ordination of poor peasants, the guerillas have spread the revolutionary flames started by Naxalbari to vast mountainous areas and plains in 12 of the country's 16 states....

The year 1970 undoubtedly witnessed the decline of the Srikakulam movement and the search by the local leadership for a correct tactical line in the place of the annihilation line sanctified as Charu Mazumdar's unique contribution to the Indian revolution, based on the blending of Lin Piao's teachings and Indian experience. The Srikakulam Regional Committee of the CPI(M-L), in a declaration in November 1970, has pledged to mobilize the peasant masses on class issues including reoccupation of land with the lords and confiscation of hoarded grain and by implication has abandoned the annihilation line albeit temporarily.[1] The declaration is also an implied repudiation of Charu Mazumdar's "revolutionary authority".

The switch in the Srikakulam units tactical line brings it closer to the Andhra Pradesh Revolutionary Communist Committee (known as the Nagi Reddy group) which has believed in coordinating class struggles with armed struggles and in coordinating other forms of struggle with armed struggle so that the majority of people could be made to participate consciously in armed struggle.[2]

The APRCC has been trying to build a guerilla zone in a contiguous forest-mountain area under its influence and has been implementing its own tactical line during the last two years. Late in December 1970, the Andhra Pradesh

---

[1] Telugu pamphlet, dated "—11-1970" and issued from "Srikakulam Struggle Area."

[2] Some Problems Concerning the Path of People's War in India, Andhra Pradesh Revolutionary Communist Committee, name of publisher or place of publication not stated, circa-mid-1970.

Government declared the Mulug, Mahaboobabad and Naras-
ampet taluks of Warangal district in the Telengana region
as "disturbed" areas, which is admission that the APRCC's
movement has acquired the dimensions of the Srikakulam
struggle in its earlier stages.

The APRCC has divided the State into areas of three
categories, based on the level of the mass movement. The
forest areas where the mass movement has reached the stages
of armed struggle, the areas where it had a wide mass base
and class struggles were intensifying; and the areas where
the mass movement was relatively weak. The APRCC
decided to take the mass movement on to the path of armed
struggle in the forest and mountainous areas; to gradually
develop mass struggles into armed struggles in the areas
where class struggles were intensifying, and to develop class
struggles in the rest of the state. Its concentration, to begin
with, was in areas where the movement could be developed
into armed struggle in a short time and thus catalyze the
revolutionary movement in the entire State.

Andhra Pradesh has a vast forest area covering thousands
of square miles on either side of the Godavari river. On
one side of the river lie the forest areas of four Telengana
districts, Khammam, Warangal, Karimnagar and Adilabad.
Across the river lie the forest areas of three coastal districts,
East Godavari, West Godavari, and Visakhapatnam. This
contiguous forest area is linked with the Srikakulam forest
by a small plain.

The forest tract chosen by the APRCC for special attention extends to Orissa, Madhya Pradesh and Maharashtra
areas and can "serve as a revolutionary base for armed struggle" in these four States.[3]

[3] Ibid.

Lakhs of Girijans live in this area, which the APRCC has been trying to develop into a guerilla zone and later a liberated zone. The Girijans are the victims of madieval feudal exploitation. The area is self-sufficient and poor in communication facilities. It also includes the area used by the Telengana guerillas as the base for their struggle in the Telengana plains during the 1946-51 peasant struggle. The people of this area have a tradition of armed struggle.

The APRCC began work in the forest tracts of Mulug taluk, where it had a mass base. Along with the propogation of revolutionary politics and armed struggle among the people, the peasants were also rallied against the exploitation by forest officials, contractors villages officials and the landlords. There was also a mobilization for occupation of forest land and the uncultivated land with the landlords. This invited resistance from the landlords which was met through squad actions, and reprisals from the Government leading to armed clashes. In areas of East Godavari district, the movement for re-occupation of lands seized by landlords achieved some success.

The movement which began in Mulug taluk has now developed in a contiguous area in seven taluks of three districts, Warangal, Khammam and Karimnagar, and to about 100 villages in East Godavari according to the APRCC. Armed attacks on the people's enemies, seizure of their moveable property and guns, burning of promissory notes and Government records with village officials, reoccupation of land seized by landlords, seizure of grain stocks for distribution among the people these are the forms of struggle used.

The lessons: "when the people's movement is advancing, wherever we lagged behind in forming armed squads to fight back landlord and police suppression, the movement has suffered a setback. And similarly, wherever we carried [out]

armed attacks without taking into consideration the level of
the people's consciousness, their political and organizational
level, the movement has suffered a setback. Wherever the
armed struggle was correctly co-ordinated with mass struggles on partial issues, the movement has advanced."[4]

The APRCC's line of co-ordinating the mass movement
and mass struggles with armed struggle does not rule out
attacks on landlords. But the difference between the
APRCC and the CPI(M-L) here is over the relationship of
such attacks with the mass movement.

Whatever the lessons drawn by the CPI(M-L) from its
Srikakulam experience, the APRCC has learnt its own
lessons. In its view, the Srikakulam armed struggle grew out
of anti-feudal struggles and the future of Srikakulam depended on co-ordination of armed struggle with a programme of
agrarian revolution. The CPI(M-L)'s claim that "red
political power" has emerged in Srikakulam are untenable
because without a regular Red army that can fight back the
regular army of the State, a red area cannot be established.
Guerilla squads cannot create a red area.

The APRCC's assessment of the annihilation line in action
in Andhra Pradesh is interesting. Militant youth in other
districts (that is, other than Srikakulam district) volunteered
to advance the cause of people's war. But instead of giving
the youth the programme for mass struggles and creation of
mass base for armed struggle, the CPI (M-L) organized
these youth into squads and asked them to carry out armed
raids against landlords.

Youth from Andhra Pradesh districts and from other
States were sent to Visakhapatnam district to implement the
annihilation tactic. The squads carried out raids without

4 *Ibid.*

any attempt to propagate the politics of armed struggle
among the people or even without establishing preliminary
contacts with the local people. All of them were arrested
soon. The experience in East Godavari has been similar.
In Guntur district, squads formed with youth from some
areas of the district carried out armed raids and took refuge
in other parts of the district. The villages where the raids
were carried out did not have any CPI(M-L) cadre and
there was no propagation of the politics of armed struggle
in these villages. In Jangaon taluk of Warangal district,
the CPI(M-L) cadre implemented the same line. In two
other districts, with the encouragement of one group of
landlords, killed two men belonging to the other group of
landlords. In Khammam district, two squads comprising
about 30 cadre carried out about 50 major and minor raids.
In Palawancha taluk, the raids took place in the plains and
the squads took shelter in the forest. There was no attempt
at political propaganda. Armed raids in the plains and shelter
in the forest was the pattern in Manukota and Illandu
taluks. No mass work or political propaganda was undertaken and the raids were indiscriminate, and even against
middle class peasants.

The raids outside Srikakulam had nothing to do with
mass work or mass issues and were not co-ordinated or conducted in a contiguous area. At best the raids reflected the
dissatisfaction and disenchantment of the idealist youth
with the parliamentary system and their determination to
attempt something new to end the system.

Thus the two tactical lines have given the Indian Maoists
two different sets of experience. One is based on a
mechanical application of Maoism, and another, on the experience of the 1946-1951 Telengana armed struggle, the
first Maoist movement in India.

CHAPTER SIX

THE POTENTIAL

INDIA IS PERHAPS the most striking focal point of the super power detente. Whatever their conflicts and contradictions elsewhere, United States and Soviet interests converge to foreclose a Maoist revolution in India. Both the super powers have a vested interest in India's stability, its parliamentary system, and its viability as a strategic Asian power to ensure continued confrontation with China. Both of them have been underwriting India to this end, with their massive economic and military aid. India's dependence on both the super powers has grown, reducing its nonalignment in foreign policy to double alignment and its public sector to bureaucrat capitalism, and helping the growth of comprador tendencies in its bourgeoisie. Neither of the super powers wants a basic solution to India's land problem and both of them are keen on promoting capitalist relations in agriculture. In the process, a serious crisis of policies has overtaken the system. The economic crisis is maturing into a political crisis rendering the system untenable. An explosive situation is building in the countryside, providing vast potential for a Maoist revolution. So Maoism is of more than academic significance for India.

India's nonalignment lapsed into double alignment with the decline of the cold war. India had all the options in a cold war situation because nonalignment gave it leverage with both the camps and it could manoeuvre successfully between them for economic and military aid. United States wanted to prevent India going communist while Soviet Union wanted to stabilize India as a nonaligned power lest it went over to the Western camp. With the easing of the cold war, nonalignment has lost its relevance. India's helplessness over Soviet military aid to Pakistan underscores this.

In the early 1950s, the Dullesian doctrine of Asians fighting Asians was the starting point of the arms race in the Indo-Pakistan subcontinent. The United States gave India economic aid, and Pakistan military aid. India was also getting Soviet economic aid and this released resources to keep India in the arms race with Pakistan. After the Sino-Indian border war in 1962, India got United States military aid while Soviet supply of hardware to India reached staggering proportions. United States discovered that Pakistan, which had been getting arms aid as part of the United States policy of containing communism, was the closest ally of China. Pakistan had begun to manoeuvre between United States and China for arms aid amidst a deterioration of Sino-Soviet relations. The 1965 Indo-Pakistani war was an epitome of the Dullesian doctrine in action. The United States decided to ban sale of lethal military equipment to both Pakistan[1] and India but the Soviet Union was quick to revive the arms race in the subcontinent. Under the pretext of weaning Pakistan away from United States and China, the Soviet Union began dumping arms on Pakistan. When India protests, the Soviet Union gives it some more hardware, to be followed by Pakistani protests. Pakistan gets more hardware. The race has been on since 1965 and

[1] The ban was removed in October 1970, despite Indian protests.

there is even reason to believe there is an implied understanding between the super powers on maintaining an arms
balance in the subcontinent. At least there is no United
States objection to growing Indian dependence on Soviet
military aid. Soviet attitude to Pakistan changed with the
Sino-Indian border war, and with the escalation of the Sino-
Soviet border conflict, there has been a perceptible change
in the Soviet attitude to South Asian countries as well (to
Iran, for example) culminating in the Brezhnev doctrine of
collective security for the region, as part of the policy of
containing China. Pakistan had to be given more arms to
wean it away from China's influence, and India, to confront
China.

Drawn into the vortex of the super power game to contain China, India has lost its options. India tried to counter
early United States aid pressures by seeking Soviet economic
aid and later using it as a lever to secure more Western aid.
But with the permanent confrontation along its land borders with both Pakistan and China, India began depending
on both the super powers. Some day the United States
might come to terms with China and pull out of South-East
Asia leaving the Soviet Union to police the region. But
Soviet pressure under economic aid to bolster India's ruling
classes, and military aid to increase its capability against
China, would stand in the way of an early solution to the
now-dormant Sino-Indian border dispute.

A third of India's federal spending goes for defence[2] and
military hardware from the Soviet Union accounts for   a
large proportion of this spending. Suffice it is to say that
all the three defence arms depend on basic Soviet equipment. The army gets its T-55 and PT-76 tanks and

2 Government of India, Budget papers 1969.

130 mm guns, etc., from the Soviet Union; the navy relies on Soviet frigates and submarines; and the air force is replacing the British and French aircraft with Sukhai-7 bombers MiG-21 interceptors and other Soviet aircraft.

Crisis of Policies

Super power aid intervention has distorted India's development and defence priorities and, consequently, to a crisis of policies. The growing political crisis is reflected in the instability of the federal government and the split in the ruling Congress Party in November 1969. Foreign aid accounted for a fifth of India's total development expenditure over its first three five year plan periods.[3] Yet the Fourth Five Year Plan was stuck for four years since 1965 due to aid uncertainties and a serious economic crisis at home. The total aid authorized from all sources during the three plans was Rs. 55,580 million, and aid utilized, Rs. 37,316 million.[4] The United States provided over half the assistance and five donors — United States, Soviet Union, the World Bank, West Germany, and United Kingdom — provided · 87 per cent of the authorized aid and 92.2 per cent of the utilized aid. Over 58 per cent of this was devoted to industrial development. While Soviet and United States aid for industrial development was widespread, assistance for vital but less profitable infrastructure section of the economy was wholly from the World Bank, the United States, and Canada. Soviet aid was distributed between industrial development (65.9 per cent) and steel and iron ore development (34.1

[3] India· Facts At a Glance, Government of India, New Delhi, 1968, p. 40.

[4] Report on Currency and Finance for the Year 1964-65, Reserve Bank of India, Bombay, 1965.

per cent), the United States (59.3 per cent of its aid was
for industrial development) made no contribution to cons-
truction of steel plants. Its credits have largely been used
for import of steel plants. While Soviet aid was 100 per
cent in the public sector, United States aid has gone to private (9.2 per cent), mixed (49.7 per cent), and public (40.8
per cent) sectors.

State planning for economic development implies state
intervention and both the super powers, besides other communist and non-communist countries, have aided India's
plans. But the objectives of state intervention in India needs
to be understood clearly. They are best judged by the results
of the three plans ending 1965. About nine-tenths of its
domestic product was still at the disposal of the private
sector and the share of the state rose by meagre 4 per
cent during the period.[5] But the share of Indian resources
in the investments made by the state has been shrinking.
During the second plan, it was 74 per cent and during the
third, it was less then 70 per cent of the investment. Thus
the state apparatus was utilized for increasing foreign aid
for public investments.[6] Another striking feature was the
phenomenal growth of the private sector over the entire
planning period because the public sector outlay on in-
frastructural assets provided the private sector with new
markets besides creating new economies.

State intervention has resulted in concentration and monopoly of economic power. As of 1963-64, the top 75 groups
of monopolies, each with minimum assets of Rs. 50 million,
owned 1,536 companies out of a total of 24,661 non-govern-
ment and non-banking companies, but their assets worked

    5 India 1966, Government of India, New Delhi, 1966, p. 150.
    6 C. Bettleim, L' Independentan, Armand Colin, Paris, 1962,
p. 210.

out at 46.9 per cent and the proportion of their paid-up
capital to that of other companies worked out to 44.1
per cent.[7] Inequalities of income have grown side by side.
A study found that 0.3 per cent of the urban population
(0.06 of the country's total population), constituting the
top bureaucrats and big business, had a fabulous living standard and controlled economic planning and development,
2 per cent of the urban population enjoyed a comfortable
standard of living, 12.1 per cent lived just above the sub-
sistance level and the rest below the subsistence line. Similarly, 0.3 per cent of the rural population (0.72 per cent of
the total population) enjoyed fabulous living standards and
served to mobilize the agricultural surpluses of another
12.2 per cent, the rest living below the subsistence level.[8]

Dependence on Soviet Union

State intervention in India has, therefore, created conditions for capitalist development, growth of monopolies,
and concentration of wealth — neither of them socialist
objectives though substantial economic aid for the intervention came from the Soviet bloc countries. The Soviet
leadership considers India a national democracy which has
chosen the non-capitalist or the middle path of development
and therefore deserved socialist economic and diplomatic
support. In India power vests in the capitalist-landlord class
alliance which can follow neither the socialist path nor
the non-capitalist class. It cannot fulfil the anti-
imperialist or anti-feudal task as the following analysis
will show.

[7] *Monopolies Inquiry Commission, Report 1965,* Government of
India, New Delhi, pp. 121-2.
[8] *Economic and Political Weekly,* 27 May 1967.

India's external liabilities have increased, its dependence
on foreign aid as a whole has grown, and foreign private
capital has made inroads into its economy during the three
plan periods and the plan holiday that followed. The an-
nual foreign exchange gap is in the order of Rs. 11,000 million.[9] Foreign obligations during the last four years were
paid out of fresh borrowings. (The total foreign debt is of
the order of Rs. 45,000 million.) The total foreign capital
invested in India has now risen to about Rs.10,000 million
and Rs. 4,389 million of non-banking investments from
private sources flowed to India between July 1948 and
December 1963.[10]

The United Kingdom and the United States supplied
over 70 per cent of the new capital that has entered India.
The most important fields in which foreign capital is en-
trenched are: petroleum refining, manufacturing including
food and beverages, textile products, transport equipment,
machinery and machine tools, metals and metal products,
electrical goods, and machinery and chemicals, etc. The
major sources of revenue for this capital is not the export market but the domestic market. The collaboration agreements relate largely to consumer goods like soft drinks, ink,
ball point pens, both paste, razor blades, and refrigerators.
Prices of machinery and accessories imported have been in-
flated to secure controlling interest in these ventures and
to conceal the real level of profits. While public loans
from foreign countries have been obtained at 2.3 to 2.5 per
cent interest, private foreign capital has been earning more

[9] V. Y. Kolhatkar, "Foreign Aid and Foreign Reliance." *Alternate
Policies for Fourth Five Year Plan*, Government of Kerala, Trivan-
drum. 1969, pp. 198-9.
[10] Michael Kidron, *Foreign Investments in India*, Oxford University Press, 1965, p. 299.

than 10 per cent of profits, in addition to royalties and fees. Of late, United States private capital has been flowing into India on a significant scale for collaboration with Indian private capital, particularly in the fertilizer industry.

The argument often invoked in India to justify the acceptance of Soviet aid is that, by strengthening the state sector, it helped India fight imperialist domination of its economy. In this context it is often contended that Soviet and communist bloc aid in general is real, disinterested aid and therefore qualitatively different from imperialist aid. Beginning with the Rs. 650 million credit in 1955 for setting up the Bhilai steel plant, Soviet aid to India has been extensive and strategic: to oil drilling, heavy engineering, coal mining, power generation, precision instruments, and electrical machinery industries. Soviet share of India's trade has also grown since 1955.

It is often pointed out that India's state sector was largely a Soviet creation. This claim is justified. The capacity installed with Soviet collaboration as a percentage of total installed capacity in the public sector industries would prove this claim: power generation, 25 per cent; power generating equipment, 70 per cent; oil extraction, 80 per cent; oil refining, 31 per cent; coal mining, 10 per cent; coal washing, 15 per cent,[11] in addition to its dominant position in the steel industry. All major products with Soviet aid were built with turn-key arrangements. Many of them have capacities unrelated to Indian needs and have piled up huge surpluses. Soviet Union has been buying some of these surpluses. Exploitation of India's cheap skilled labour and raw material has been the Soviet objective because some of

[11] *Liberation*, February 1969.

the latest collaboration proposals are: branch   industries
(where Indo-Soviet factories, using Soviet machinery and
raw materials will make goods which are to be sent back
to Soviet Union), export industries (Indo-Soviet collaboration to produce goods exclusively for export to third countries), and third country joint ventures (which would utilize machinery and equipment produced   in   Soviet-aided
Indian projects).

In the place of the old imperialism which took primary
products to the metropolitan country and exported manufactured primary products back to the colony, colonial exploitation of India is taking a new form, through an intri-
cate control of certain types of industries.   This gives the
aid giver profit on sale of capital equipment, use of cheap
labour, and use of the country as base to capture both internal markets and markets in less developed countries, and
in the process political control of the aid receiving country.

The state sector in India, built largely with Soviet bloc aid,
has only helped the Indian bourgeoisie to collaborate on a
larger scale with monopolies and turn comprador.

Thus, not only is the Indian bourgeoisie not capable of
completing the anti-imperialist task but has been halting
in its anti-feudal task, compromising with feudalism in many
forms. The result is an explosive situation in the countryside. Gunnar Myrdal in his *Asian Drama* observed that the
Indian village is "like a complex molecule among   whose
parts extreme tensions have built up.   Although the tensions criss-cross in a manner that maintains equilibrium, it
is conceivable that they might reorganise in a way   that
would explode the molecule. This probably   would   not
happen spontaneously, but as a result of the forceful onslaught from outside."

Unquiet Countryside

In the sprawling countryside today what are described as
agrarian tensions is nothing but class struggle. A new
technology is being tried on an outmoded agrarian structure adding to the social and political tensions. The new
technology that has gone into India's "green revolution"
and a strong Maoist movement among the peasantry might
well turn out to be the twin forces that would provide the
"forceful onslaught from outside" Myrdal spoke of. Already
the situation is explosive and India's Home Minister, Y. B.
Chavan, grimly warned in November 1969: "Unless the
Green Revolution is accompanied by a revolution based on
social justice, I am afraid the Green Revolution may not
remain green."[12]

A study of the agrarian agitations in 1966-69 by the Indian Home Ministry came to the disquieting conclusion
that "a bad agricultural season could lead to an explosive
situation in the rural areas,"[13] because the persistence of
serious social and economic inequalities resulted in serious
tensions. The agitations generally related to distribution of
land to landless, wages of farm labour, and security of tenure.
The forms ranged from Gandhian satyagraha (passive resistance) to strikes and, sometimes, armed clashes. The
massive land grab movement in July-August 1970 turned
the spotlight on the growing land hunger and the explosive
situation in the countryside, confirming the findings of the
study that certain political parties had succeeded in pockets
in organizing landless labour, poor peasants and others with

[12] Quoted in Link, 18 January 1970.
[13] Research and Policy Division, Ministry of Home Affairs, Government of India, The Causes and Nature of Current Agrarian
Tensions, 1969, unpublished monograph, pp. 13.

insecure tenancies; and that the agitation for distribution
of land to the landless had good response and a wide geo-
graphical spread.

The growing land hunger is underlined by the decline
in the cultivable waste land, from eight per cent in 1950-51
to 5.6 per cent in 1965-66, with the area not available for
cultivation remaining steady around 16.5 per cent. The
net areas sown during the period has risen by a meagre three
per cent from 41.8. Population pressure on land has been
growing, the per capita sown area declining from 0.99 acre
in 1951 to 0.89 acre in 1964. During the same period, agricultural holdings below five acres rose from 22 million to
32 million and average size of holdings shrank from 7.5
acres to 6.5.

About 49 per cent of the national income comes from
the agricultural sector which accounts for 70 per cent of the
working population. The 1961 census returned 99.6 million
as cultivators and 31.5 million as agricultural labourers. Thus
the work force in agriculture (which includes both cultivators and agricultural labourers) accounts for 134.3 million
out of the total work force of 162.3 million. Among agricultural workers, the more numerous category, cultivators,
increased from 69.7 million in 1951 to 99.6 million in 1961,
an increase of 43.0 per cent. The percentage to total workers went up from 50 to 52.8 per cent. Agricultural labour,
that is, those who sustain themselves mainly from wage
employment in agriculture, increased from 27.5 million in
1951 to 31.5 million in 1961 — an increase of 14.5 per
cent.

Land reform legislation since India's Independence in
1947 broadly aimed at eliminating feudal relations by doing
away with intermediaries and bringing the agriculturist in
direct relationship with the state, providing security to the

tenants, checking concentration of land through ceilings on ownership, resettlement of landless agricultural labour and consolidation of fragmented holdings and reorganization of the small farm economy. In tangible terms, the land reforms eliminated intermediaries in 40 per cent of the area under zamindari, jagirdari, and inamdari areas, which were brought under the ryotwari system. The 1961 census reported that less than 2.75 per cent of the tenures were non-ryotwari. Over 30 million tenants of former intermediaries have now been brought into direct (ryotwari) relationship with the state. About 10 million areas of land is claimed to have been distributed to the landless. Collection of land revenue which in the past had been an inelastic source, has gone up from Rs. 780 million in 1965-66 to Rs. 1,200 million in 1965-66. Over three million tenants and sharecroppers have acquired ownership in over seven million acres. As a result of the ceiling on land holdings, two million acres have been declared surplus and over half of it distributed. Consolidation of holdings has progressed considerably in most States.

But as an official study admits, "agrarian reforms which made an enthusiastic start immediately after Independence have almost ground to a halt,"[14] and the laws have been circumvented with impunity. About 82 per cent of tenants do not enjoy fixity of tenure and are either tenants at will or subject to landlords right to resumption, or enjoy at best temporary protection. Land has been leased on large scale even in areas where intermediary tenures do not obtain and land has been sub-leased where such tenures existed. These problems have survived the abolition of intermediaries. In law, "personal cultivation" is defined so vaguely that there has been large-scale eviction of tenants on the ground that

[14] *Ibid.,* p. 3.

the landlord wants to resume land for personal cultivation. Where law was passed to check this, evictions have been taking place in the guise of "voluntary surrenders." There has been no material change in the conditions of agricultural labour and the minimum wages legislation "remains a dead letter because wages fixed about 8 or 10 years ago have not been revised."[15] Thus vestiges of feudalism have survived 22 years of Independence because state policy aimed at promoting capitalist relations in land has been halting and ineffective because the bourgeoisie has been forced to make compromises with feudal interests.

Price of Green Revolution

Kulakization of agriculture is a new trend resulting from the new technology in agriculture with state support. The strategy, production oriented to reduce India's heavy dependence on imported food, was evolved in 1965. It is based on a systematic effort to extend the application of science and technology, including better inputs and more scientific methods to raise yields. The outcome of the application of the new technology is described as a breakthrough, a Green Revolution. Agricultural production has increased from around 50 million tonnes at the time of Independence to 88.4 million tonnes in 1964-65 and after two years of severe drought, shot up to 96 million tonnes in 1968-69. This is largely the function of technology and as an official study says "it is possible for even a three acre farm to become a surplus unit and even this is only a rough guide to its great potentialities in the future."[16]

[15] Quoted in *ibid.* from National Labour Commission's "Diagonistic Study of Conditions of Rural Labour."
[16] *Ibid.*, p. 2.

But the new strategy aimed at solving the food problem and not the land problem. As admitted by the official study:

The interests of what might be called the agricultural classes have not converged on commonly accepted set of social and economic objectives ... the new technology and strategy having been geared to goals of production, with secondary regard to social imperatives, have brought about a situation in which elements of disparity, instability and unrest are becoming conspicuous with the possibility of increase in tensions.[17]

Another study, undertaken for the United States Agency for International Development, has underlined this more forcefully. The case studies reveal that all classes of cultivators have experienced some improvement in income and yield from the new technology. This is particularly true of the wheat growing areas. It is also certain that gains of the new technology have been unevenly distributed, the big farmers gaining proportionately more than the small farmers. In fact, where small farmers also take part of their holdings on lease, or are pure tenants, the rising rentals resulting from the rise in land values and or the tendency of land owners to resume land for personal cultivation because of the high returns farming with new technology offers, there has been a deterioration in the condition of this class of farmers. Farmers with holdings of five and ten acres have done better but only a small percentage of farmers with 10 acres of more have been able to command the capital needed for land development to make the best use of the new technology. Farmers with 20 acres and more have

[17] *Ibid.*, p. 2-3.

gained most, both absolutely and relatively.

Majority of farmers — probably 75 to 80 per cent in the rice belt — have been hard hit by the introduction of new technology. The reason is the new programme has been

> ... introduced into a setting where economic disparities have already been substantially sharpened by the differential capacity of small and large farmers, and tenants and landowners to sustain capital outlays on land development, especially minor irrigation, and other modern equipment that are necessary to realize the full benefits of the new technology.[18]

In rice growing areas, the economic polarization as a result of the Green Revolution is marked between the large farmers on one hand and the majority of small holders on the other, between owner-cum-tenant cultivators and the share-croppers on the other. The small farmers have not derived proportionate benefits but have even suffered deterioration.

There is not only economic polarization, but social estrangment, as the USAID study notes. Rural economy is no longer a subsistence way of life but profitable investment, as the spurt in rentals proves. The land reform laws, which the study says have largely been "abortive" have caused land owners to look at the tenants as potential adversaries, and eroded the traditional attitudes of interdependence.

In the earlier stages, the Green Revolution might appear profitable to the landless labour because with more intensive farming and a diversified cropping pattern, the demand for labour might go up. But already, the machine is making itself felt. There is growing demand for tractors and

very soon the harvester-combines will make their appearance in the Indian farms, displacing labour, when the labour force itself is expanding creating a vast rural proletariat.
As the study says:

> The situation is potentially all the more serious because
> Leftist parties openly proclaim their intention of trans-
> forming these tendencies towards economic and social
> polarization into open political confrontation between the
> minority of prosperous landowners, and the great majority
> of sharecroppers and landles labourers.
>
> It is unfortunate for India, but nevertheless true, that the
> greatest technological possibilities for increasing produc-
> tion should have come about precisely at a time when
> traditional solidarity structures are badly weakened, when
> social resentment about increasing disparities is at a new
> height, and when Leftist political parties are increasingly
> active (and successful) in mobilizing social discontent for
> a radical goal.[19]

The economic polarization resulting from the Green Revolution will be sharpened by the bourgeois-democratic land
reforms the state now proposes to bring about capitalist land
relations by eliminating the vestiges of feudalism. In effect,
there will be a polarization of property relations, eliminating the middle class as a factor in politics and the rich peasant who stands to benefit most by the new technology has
already emerged as a strategic class in the Indian political
system. Every political party that belongs to the system
has to rely on this class. If the growing army of rural proletariat is not absorbed in the secondary and tertiary sectors,

---

[18] Francine Frankel, "Agricultural Modernization and Social
Change," *Mainstream*, 29 November 1969.

the confrontation in the countryside will be fiercer than it would otherwise be.

The New Kulaks

Both the super powers are keen on promoting capitalist land relations in India. Every fourth tractor in the country is Soviet-made and socialist bloc countries (Poland and Czechoslovakia) account for high percentage of the tractor production capacity. East Germany has been another source of tracter supplies. Tractorization of agriculture has promoted large-scale capitalist farming and promises large-scale displacement of agricultural labour. It demands land reforms aimed at eliminating the remnants of feudalism and concentrating agricultural surpluses in a new class of rich peasants or kulaks who would opt for higher technology in farming. Kulakization of farming would be in the Soviet interest but not a more fundamental solution to India's land problem. Soviet stake in India's parliamentary system makes this new kulak class a strategic force which would compel the support of both the super powers.

The "new agricultural strategy" owes its inspiration to the Ford Foundation's "package programme" for agriculture and the High Yielding Varieties Programme (also of United States inspiration). Larger inputs of chemical fertilizer and the use of insecticides and pesticides are part of the new strategy. The expanding fertilizer needs to meet India's food gap increases India's dependence on United States and other advanced countries. Either India has to import fertilizer or plants to produce fertilizer. The recent liberalization of industrial policy to permit the participation of pri-

19 Ibid.

vate United States capital in fertilizer production is direct proof of this dependence. It is in the interest of United States private capital to prop the new agricultural strategy and to urge the implementation of land reform legislation so that capitalist relations would grow in agriculture.

Participation in the parliamentary system makes it impossible for any political party to alienate the strategic rich peasant class by relying on the landpoor and landless peasant, and the agricultural labourer. The emergence of the new class of rich peasants has weakened central planning and central authority and defeated the resources mobilization effort because no government dare tax this class which has stood to gain most from state support to agriculture... Only a party that functions outside the parliamentary system and does not need the support of the new class at the elections can direct its appeal to the landless and landpoor peasants and the growing rural proletariat.

Herein lies the challenge to the Indian Maoist movement. The passivity and non-violent nature of the Indian peasant is a myth. He has risen in revolt again and again without any political direction and the revolts were suppressed. If the Maoist movement discovers its idiom of revolution and organizes the large, growing rural proletariat which cannot be absorbed in industry through capitalist development, a critical confrontation will develop. India will witness a rash of agrarian agitations in scattered pockets and if the Maoists give these movements political direction, co-ordinate and link them up the movements would grow into a mass peasant upsurge with a countrywide spread. Vast revolutionary potential has existed in India for quite some time and the interaction of a Maoist movement on this potential might well trigger off the explosion of the "complex molecule" that the Indian village is.

Whether the Indian Maoist movement would prove equal to the challenge is an open question. The problem before it has been one of correct linkage between strategy and tactics. The tactical problems include the relationship between the petit bourgeois leadership of the movement and the rural and urban masses, the identification of the principal contradiction and the main enemy; the linkage between the struggles of the urban masses and the rural masses; and the linkage between various forms of struggle.

SELECT BIBLIOGRAPHY

DOCUMENTS/AUTHORITATIVE STATEMENTS

A Proposal Concerning the General Line of the International Communist Movement, Central Committee of the Communist Party of China, 14 June 1963.

Andhra Letter, June 1948, unpubished.

Andhra Plenum Rejects Neo-Revisionist Ideological Draft, Janasakthi publication, Vijayawada, 1968.

Communique of the Afro-Asian Writers Emergency Meeting, Peking, 9 July 1966, People's Daily, 15 July 1966.

Concerning the Problems of the Path of People's War in India, Andhra Pradesh Revolutionary Communist Committee, 1970.

Constitution of the Communist Party of India (Marxist-Leninist), May 1970, mimeographed.

Election Review and Party's Tasks, Communist Party of India (Marxist), 1967.

Immediate Programme, Andhra Pradesh Revolutionary Communist Committee, 1966 mimeographed.

"On Agrarian Question in India," Politbureau document, Communist, February 1947.

On Differences With the All-India Co-ordination Committee of Communist Revolutionaries, Maharashtra State Co-ordination Committee of Communist Revolutionaries, resolution 15 June 1968.

"On the Indian Situation and Our Immediate Task," All-India Co-ordination Committee of Communist Revolutionaries, Liberation, November 1968.

On Left Deviation and Left Opportunism, Resolution of the Central Committee of the Communist Party of India (Marxist), Madurai, 18-27 August 1967.

"On People's Democracy," Politbureau document, Communist, June-July 1949.

On Srikakulam Girijan Armed Struggle, Andhra Pradesh Revolutionary Communist Committee, 1969, mimeographed.

Lin Piao, "Long Live the Victory of People's War," People's Daily, 2 September 1965; Peking Review, 3 September 1965.

On Telengana, Information document no. 7 (2) by an unidentified member of the Andhra Committee of the CPI, 1950, mimeographed.

Open Letter to Party Members, Tarimela Nagi Reddy, Devulapalli
    Venkateswara Rao, Kollah Venkiah, and Chandra Pulla
    Reddy, Vijayawada 1969.
"Political Resolution," Communist Party of India (Marxist-Leninist),
    Liberation, May 1969.
Problems of People's War, Andhra Pradesh Revolutionary Com-
    munist Committee, 1969, mimeographed.
Programme of the Communist Party of India (Marxist), Calcutta,
    1965.
Programme of the Communist Party of India (Marxist-Leninist),
    May 1970, mimeographed.
Resolution of Andhra State Committee, All-India Co-ordination
    Committee of Communist Revolutionaries, 7 February 1969,
    Liberation, March 1969.
Resolution on Elections, All-India Co-ordination Committee of
    Communist Revolutionaries, *Liberation*, June 1968.
Resolution on Party Organisation, Communist Party of India
    (Marxist-Leninist), May 1970, mimeographed.
Sanyal, Kanu, "Report on Peasant Struggle in the Terai Region,"
    Liberation, November 1968.
"Speech by Liu Shao-chi at the Conference of Trade Unions of
    Asia, Australaia and Oceania," *For a Lasting Peace, For a
    People's Democracy*, 30 December 1949.
"Spring Thunder Over India," *People's Daily*, 5 July 1967.
*Struggle for People's Democracy and Socialism—Some Questions of
    Strategy and Tactics*, Politbureau of the CPI, *Communist*,
    June-July 1949.
Revolutionary Peasant Struggle in Debra, West Bengal, Report by
    Debra Thana Organising Committee, CPI (M-L), *Liberation*,
    December 1969.
"Statement of the Editorial Board," *Communist*, February-March
    1950.
"Statement of the Editorial Board on the Anti-Leninist Criticism of
    Comrade Mao Tse-tung," *Communist*, February-March 1950.
*The Origin and Development of Differences Between the Leadership
    of the CPSU and Ourselves*, Comment on the Open Letter of
    the Central Committee of the CPSU, *Peking Review*, 13 Sep-
    tember 1963.
Tactical Line, unpublished document circulated to delegates at the
    Third Congress of the Communist Party of India, Madurai
    1953.

ARTICLES

"After the Indian Elections: A Still More Reactionary Government,"
    Peking Review, 24 March 1967.
"Apologists for Neo-colonialism," *Peking Review*, 25 October 1963.
Basavapunniah, M., "Our Party's Stand on Naxalbari," *People's
    Democracy*, 9 July 1967.

BIBLIOGRAPHY

Commentator, "Let the Peasant Revolutionary Storm in India Strike Harder," Peking Review, 1 March 1968.

Commentator, "Let the Red Flag of Naxalbari Fly Still Higher," People's Daily, 7 August 1967, Peking Review, 13 August 1967.

"Dange's Plot to Sabotage Indian People's Revolution Will Surely Fail," People's Daily, 4 June 1967, Peking Review, 9 June 1967.

"Flames of Guerilla Struggle Spreads to New Areas," Liberation, December 1969.

"Flames of People's War Burn Brightly in Srikakulam," Liberation, August 1969.

"Great New Era of World Revolution," Peking Review, 13 January 1967.

"Imperialist Camp Enters a Gloomy New Year," Peking Review, 20 January 1967.

"India: Anti-tyranny Struggles Rock Reactionary Rule," Peking Review, 24 February 1967.

"Indian People Rise Up in Resistance," Peking Review, 18 November 1966.

"Indian Revolutionary Armed Struggle Surges Forward," Peking Review, reprinted in Liberation, December 1969.

"Lessons of the Telengana Peasants Armed Struggle," NCNA, Peking, 2 August 1967.

Mazumdar, Charu, "A Few Words to the Revolutionary Students and Youths," Liberation, March 1970.

———, "Make the 1970's the Decade of Liberation," Liberation, February 1970.

———, "March Forward by Summing Up the Experience of the Peasant Revolutionary Struggle of India," Liberation, December 1969.

———, "On Some Current Political and Organisational Problems," Liberation, July 1969.

———, "One Year of Naxalbari," Liberation, June 1968.

———, "The Peasant Revolutionary Struggle in Srikakulam is Invincible," Liberation, March 1970.

———, "To My Comrades," Liberation, October 1968.

Observer, "To Win Victory in the Revolution We Must Establish the Revolutionary Authority," Liberation, February 1970.

"Our Path: Guerilla Warfare," Liberation, November 1969.

"Red Area of Revolutionary Struggle Expands in Andhra Despite Campaign of Suppression," Liberation, July 1969.

"Red Revolutionary Area in India Shines Like a Beacon," Peking Review, reprinted in Liberation, February 1970.

"Reports on Uttar Pradesh and Bihar," Liberation, July 1969.

"Report of Srikakulam," Liberation, May 1969.

"Revolutionary Struggle of the Indian People Grows in Depth," Peking Review, 31 January 1969.

Shish Yen, "Non-aligned India's Double Alignment," Peking Review, 13 August 1965.

"Student Movement in India," Peking Review, 2 December 1966.

"Srikakulam Going the Way Predicted by Charu Mazumdar," *Liberation*, September 1969.

"Srikakulah Guerilla Struggle Extends to the Plains—A Lesson," *Liberation*, November 1969.

"Srikakulam Marches On," *Liberation*, April 1969.

"Srikakulam Struggle Continues to Spread and Develop," *Liberation*, June 1960.

"The Militant Banner of Afro-Asian Solidarity is Flying High," Editorial, *People's Daily*, 10 July 1966; *Peking Review*, 15 July 1967.

Ting Chuan, "Food Crisis and Why," *Peking Review*, 11 March 1966.

"The Revolutionary Girijans are Learning Warfare Through Warfare," *Liberation*, February 1969.

"The Revolutionary Working Class Party is Born," *Liberation*, May 1969.

INDEX